The Amazing Journey Ser...

"Beginnings"

"The story of God's sovereign choices
and man's sinful choices in Genesis"

Published by Createspace, a division of Amazon

ISBN-13: 978-1495353611

ISBN-10: 1495353613

February 2014

ACKNOWLEDGMENTS

I could not write without the help of many people. First, I thank the Lord for giving me the opportunity to study His word and the Holy Spirit for giving me a passion to teach the truth. In spite of many failures, God has been faithful as He promised, and I praise Him for His grace every day.

Second, I thank my wife, Kay, who has patiently endured (most of the time) my hours in the study, researching Scripture, writing, thinking, and praying for divine help. She often plays "Word" games while I write.

Third, a special thanks to my sister-in-law, Carol, who faithfully and patiently proof reads my books to find those errors that I miss. And there are many! Thank you Carol.

And last, a special thanks to my professors ,who years ago helped me to appreciate the importance of God's word, and to my friends who endure my incessant talk about what I am writing and give me ideas for improvement.

To God alone be the glory. All errors in grammar, spelling, and theology are mine alone, but the Living God is perfect, holy and just. Listen carefully to His word, and judge my words by His word.

INTRODUCTION TO

"The Amazing Journey Series'

The Bible is a most interesting book. Understandably, many people do not like to read the Old Testament because they do not understand it. However, the Old Testament is God's "picture book" and describes how God works in the lives of people and nations. The New Testament, on the other hand, beginning with the Book of Romans, is more of a doctrinal explanation of God's plan. Because I have heard this complaint about not understanding the Old Testament from so many people over the years, I have always told people that understanding the Old Testament is essential for understanding the New Testament.

I wrote my very first book, "The Story of Salvation," at the suggestion of a friend and never intended to write another book. However, before I finished it, I decided to do a series on the entire Bible to help people understand the flow of the Bible. "Salvation" became volume 9 in the series, and since I had indicated in the last chapter of "The Story of Salvation" that the next message series was on the Book of Revelation, I wrote "EPILOGUE: The Consummation of God's Eternal Plan." "EPILOGUE" became volume 10 in the series.

I recently read several books about the story of the Bible and I watched 'The Bible' series on television. While these are good attempts to help people understand the Bible, I finished each book and the TV series thinking that "something was missing." So it is my desire in this series is to capture that "something missing" part, and put together volumes that help the reader to understand not just the content of the Bible, but the flow of the Bible as it relates to God's overall plan. The beauty of the Bible is that it is one cohesive unity. From Genesis to Revelation God's word tells one story— God's plan for mankind.

I have often told people that you can start with any verse in Scripture and tell the entire story of God's plan from that starting point. Let me give two illustrations where that happened in Scripture. Remember the two disciples that met Jesus on the road to Emmaus after the resurrection? They didn't recognize Jesus, but as they talked with Him they related how they had hoped that Jesus was the expected Messiah. Jesus responded,

> "And He said to them, "O foolish men and slow of heart to believe in all that the prophets have spoken! "Was it not necessary for the Christ to suffer these things and to enter into His glory?" Then beginning with Moses and with all the prophets, He explained to them the things concerning Himself in all the Scriptures." Luk 24:25-27.[1]

Jesus started in the Pentateuch and went through the Old Testament explaining Himself to these two men. Wouldn't you have liked to have been there to hear Jesus summarize the Old Testament Scriptures?

---

[1] All Biblical references are from the 1995 NASB copied from e-sword Bible study program

The apostle Phillip taught about Jesus to the Ethiopian eunuch in Acts 8. Listen to what Phillip said when he found the man was reading Isaiah 53.

> Then Philip opened his mouth, and beginning from this Scripture he preached Jesus to him. As they went along the road they came to some water; and the eunuch *said, "Look! Water! What prevents me from being baptized?" Act 8:35-36.

Starting in Isaiah 53 Phillip preached Jesus from the Old Testament just like Jesus did on the road to Emmaus! He explained how to be saved, and he explained about baptism by immersion for believers— from the Old Testament! The eunuch asked to be baptized and Phillip baptized him.

> "And he ordered the chariot to stop; and they both went down into the water, Philip as well as the eunuch, and he baptized him. When they came up out of the water, the Spirit of the Lord snatched Philip away; and the eunuch no longer saw him, but went on his way rejoicing." Act 8:37-39

According to the historian, Eusebius, the eunuch went home and became a witness for Christ.[2]

The first 8 volumes of this series will summarize the content of Scripture as it relates to and advances God's plan. I will include those events which are significant to God's plan of redemption, but at the same time, I will summarize the difficult parts of Scripture to give an overview of why God includes them in Scripture and what their importance is in God's plan Following is a summary of the content of those volumes.[3]

1- "Beginnings-"   - the story of Genesis

---

[2] http://www.ccel.org/ccel/schaff/npnf201.iii.vii.ii.html

[3] Volumes 2-8 have not yet been written.

2- "Foundations-"	- the study of the growth of Israel in the books of Exodus through Joshua
3- "Rebellion-"	- the story of rebellious Israel in the books of Judges, Ruth, 1 Sam.1-8
4- "United-"	- the story of the Monarchy under the rule of Saul, David, and Solomon
5- "Divided-"	- the story of the divided nation
6- "Conquered-"	- the story of the captivity of the Northern and Southern tribes
7- "Rebuilding-"	- the story of the return to the land and rebuilding of the temple and the wall under the leaderships of Ezra and Nehemiah
8- "Set aside - Replaced"	- the story of Israel's rejection of Christ, their Messiah and the spread of the gospel in the Gospels, Acts and Epistles

Volumes 9 and 10 are theological novels and because they contain information about situations and people in the first church I served. I chose not to reveal the location or identify of the church. Therefore, I wrote those books under a pen name: Pastor John Davis. However, since the process of writing the remaining books of the series will take quite some time, I have decided to write the first eight volumes under my own name. While names and places have been changed, it is my desire that the stories in volumes 9 and 10 not offend anyone connected with the church. Following is a summary of those volumes.

9- "The Story of	- the story of God's sovereign work to Salvation-"save His sheep
10- "Epilogue- The	- the study of the Book of Revelation the Consummation of God's Eternal Plan"

My prayer is that this series will not only help you to understand God's plan in the Bible, but will also stimulate a love for the Old Testament that results in further study for your own spiritual growth. God's wonderful plan begins with Creation and ends with a new creation; it begins with man's sin and ends with man's salvation; it begins with Satan deceiving Eve and ends with Eve's descendent, Jesus Christ, defeating Satan forever. Our God has a plan that He is working out in this world. Where do you fit in that plan? Will you be forever with Christ, the Redeemer, or forever with Satan, the deceiver, in the Lake of Fire that God prepared for the devil and his demons?

The charts on the next 2 pages give a more detailed overview of the proposed content of each of the books.

Overview of the 'Amazing Journey Series' (Cont.)

Volume	6	7	8	9	10
Title	"Conquered"	'Rebuilding'	'Set Aside'	'Salvation'	'Epilogue'
Books	2 Kgs.24,25, 2 Chron. 10-36 Prophets	Ezra / Nehemiah	Gospels to Jude	Bible	Revelation
Content	1. **North:** 10 tribes enslaved by Assyria in 722 B.C. 2. **South:** 2 tribes enslaved by Babylon in 586 B.C.	1. **The Temple** under Ezra 2. **The Wall** under Nehemiah	1. **Israel rejected** temporarily by their Messiah • Israel rejected their Messiah (Mk.8.31) • The Messiah rejected Israel (Mt.21.43) 2. **Israel replaced** temporarily by the Body of Christ • Understood by the apostles • Unbelief brought salvation to the Gentiles • Until the last Gentile is saved	1. **God's choice** in eternity past to save some • **Cursed** by Adam's sin • **Condemned** to separation • **Completely helpless** to save ourselves 2. **God's Christ** in time and space securing salvation for those God chose • **Conviction** by the Holy Spirit • **Conversion** by the Holy Spirit	1. **The Rapture** of the Body of Christ 2. **The Redemp-tion** of Israel 3. **The Revelation** of Jesus Christ 3. **The Retribution** to the wicked 4. **The Restoration** of the Kingdom to Israel 5. **The Reconstruc-tion** of the earth

Overview of the 'Amazing Journey Series'

Volume	1	2	3	4	5
Title	'Beginnings"	"Foundations"	"Rebellion"	"United"	'Divided'
Books	Genesis	Exodus to Joshua	Judges/Ruth	1 Sam.13.1-31.3, 1 Kgs.1-11.43	1 Kgs.12.1-22.53, 2 Kgs.1.1-25.30, 2 Chronicles 10.1-36.23
Content	1. **Creation** • Universe • Humans 2. **Corruption** • Physical • Moral • Spiritual 3. **Condemnation** • Physical death • Spiritual death • Eternal death 4. **Covenants** • **Noah:** sign of a rainbow > No universal floods > Sign: rainbow • **Abraham:** sign of circumcision > A great nation > A land of their own > A blessing to the world	1. **Independence** • Deliverance from Egypt • Destination to their new land 2. **Instructions** • The Moral law • The Civil law • The Ceremonial law 3. **Insurrection** • 10 Complaints that test God's patience • 10 collaborators that bring God's punishment for 40 years 4. **Inheritance** • God: The Levites • The Eleven tribes: Land • Levites: God, cities, tithes, and portions of the sacrifices	1. **A Cycle** • Rebellion • Repentance • Restoration 2. **A Commitment** • Ruin • Reunion • Redemption 3. **A Condition** • **Acceptable:** Idolatry and kidnapping • **Acceptable:** Immorality and killing	1. **Saul:** a weak king disapproved by God 2. **David:** a worshiping king dedicated to God 3. **Solomon:** a wise king distracted by foreign wives	1. **South:** 2 tribes with 5 good kings out of 19 kings 2. **North:** 10 tribes with 19 evil kings

May God bless you as you read this first book in the series. It is my pray that you will understand that the sovereign God who created all things is worthy of your honor, praise, and submission to His plan for your life. The Bible is about God; all of life is about God and His glory; it is not about us and our desires. Should you desire to read the first two published volumes, you may purchase a print book from Amazon,[1] or an ebook for the Kindle. Those two volumes also have study guides which are available only in printed form from Amazon.

---

[1] Search for Pastor John Davis on Amazon/ and Kindle to find the books

OUTLINE OF GENESIS

"Beginnings"

"The story of God's sovereign choices and
man's sinful choices in Genesis"

(Book 1 of "The Amazing Journey Series")

I.   Creation

    A. Preliminary matters

        1. The Case against Evolution
        2. The Case for Creation

    B. The Genesis record on God's methods

        1. Ex Nihilo
        2. Instantaneously
        3. In an orderly way
        4. In six 24-hour days
        5. Fully mature

II.   Corruption and condemnation

    A. The temptation of Satan
    B. The consequences of sin: corruption and death

        1. The Immediate consequences for Adam and Eve

            a. Sin with its shame
            b. Spiritual death
            c. Physical death
            d. Expulsion from the Garden
            e. Toil, trouble and pain,
            f. Pain in child-bearing
            g. Difficulties in the marriage relationship

2. The curse upon the serpent and Satan

3. Continuing consequences of death for the human race

    a. Physical death
    b. Spiritual
    c. Eternal

III. Covenants

A. The covenant with Noah (Gen.5-10)

    1. The universal flood
    2. Sign of the rainbow

B. The covenant with Abraham (Gen.11-50)

    1. The covenant instituted (Gen.11-20)

        a. Abraham's suggestion to God
        b. Sarah's sinful attempt to fulfill the covenant

    2. The cutting of the covenant

        a. The sign of the covenant: circumcision
        b. The significance of the covenant summarized

            (1) To become a great nation
            (2) To have a land of their own
            (3) To bless the world

    3. The covenant fulfilled (Gen.21-50, Rev.20)

        a. The initial fulfillment of the covenant (Gen.21-50)

            (1) Through Isaac

                (a) The birth and sacrifice of Isaac
                (b) The confirmation of the covenant to Isaac

       (c) Isaac's marriage to Rebekah and his
          sons Esau and Jacob

          1) His marriage
          2) The birth of Esau and Jacob

(2) Through Jacob

       (a) The covenant reaffirmed through Jacob
       (b) Jacob's flight to Laban\

          1) His marriage to Leah
          2) His marriage to Rachel
          3) His mistreatment by Laban

       (c) His reunion with Esau
       (d) The reaffirmation of God's covenant
          (Gen.35)

       (e) Jacob's move to Egypt

          1) Joseph sent ahead to prepare a place
          2) Israel grows into a great nation

   b. The final fulfillment: the Millennial king dom
      (Rev.20)

Summary

"BEGINNINGS"

"The story of God's sovereign choices and man's sinful choices in Genesis"

INTRODUCTION

Genesis is the book of 'Beginnings' and 'firsts.' Creation, sin, the Fall of man, the first marriage, the first murder, the first rapture, the first rain, the first destruction of the earth, the first rainbow and the beginning of the nation of Israel are just a few of the 'beginnings' and 'firsts.' We learn in Genesis how a sovereign God chose to create the universe and His purpose for it. Unfortunately, we also learn in Genesis that God's highest creation, man,

Overview of Genesis

GENESIS

Major Events	Significance of the events
1. Creation	Beginning of history
2. Fall of man	Beginning of sin / judgment
3. Flood	Beginning of changed geography
4. Babel	Beginning of languages
5. Obedience of Abraham	Beginning of the nation of Israel
6. Imprisonment of Joseph	Beginning of God's protection of Israel

chose to sin rather than obey God, and all mankind now suffers the consequences of that sin.

Genesis is also a book about choices; God's sovereign choices and man's sinful choices. The chart below gives an over-

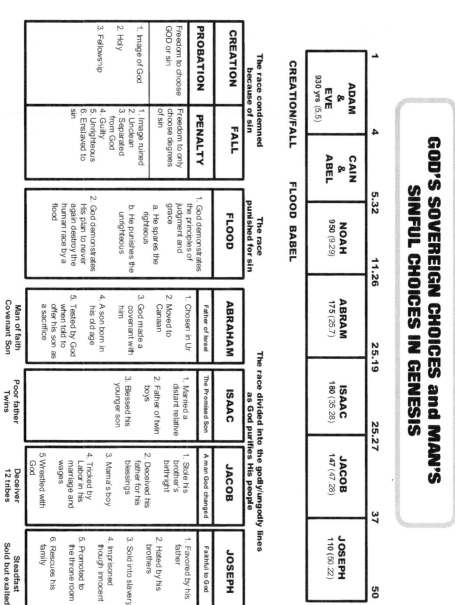

view of those choices. We learn that God makes sovereign choices based upon His own will; man makes sinful choices based upon his sinful nature. God chose to create the universe; He chose to create man; He chose to test man; He chose to save some from the sinful race; He chose to favor one nation above all others; He chose to start that nation through Abraham; and He sent Joseph ahead to prepare a place where that nation could grow to large numbers safely. God orchestrates history according to His purposes; He sovereignly uses whomever He chooses. Life is about God and His glory; it is about the outworking of God's plan; it is not about us.

Man chose sin instead of obedience to God; he chose to murder, chose to build a tower toward heaven, and chose to rebel against God in many different ways. Sinful man desires to go his own way, and even those who believed in God struggled against the temptations to sin.

The warfare between God and Satan, and between good and evil continues to this day. Genesis shows us the beginning of this warfare, and the beginning of God's remedy for sin. The remainder of the Bible fills in the details of God's plan to provide redemption for sinful man. The chart on the next page shows God's plan to to bring Christ the Redeemer through the nation of Israel.

Genesis begins the outworking of God's plan to redeem man through Jesus Christ who comes through the line of Abraham and David, presents Himself as Israel's Messiah, but is rejected, crucified, then rises from the grave, and ascends to heaven to wait until the last Gentile is saved. Then Christ will return in power and glory

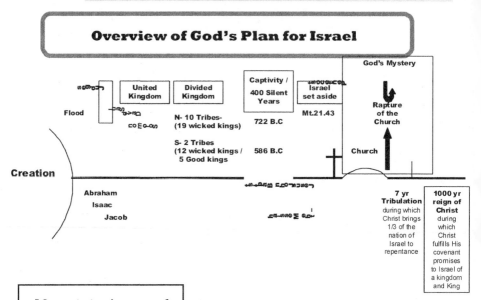

to set up the kingdom promised to Abraham.

> "Genesis is also one of the most attacked books of the Bible, but rest assured, there has never been a successful attack against Genesis that has stood the test of time and the spade."

Genesis is also one of the most attacked books of the Bible, but rest assured, there has never been a successful attack against Genesis that has stood the test of time and the spade. To deny the authenticity of Genesis is to deny the authenticity of the remainder of Scripture, and to deny the veracity of Jesus Christ who quoted or referred to historical events in Genesis frequently. If Jesus Christ accepted the book of Genesis as authentic, then we must also accept it as authentic. Here are just a few examples of Jesus quoting or referring to historical events Genesis.

> "...and said, 'FOR THIS REASON A MAN SHALL LEAVE HIS FATHER AND MOTHER AND BE JOINED TO HIS WIFE, AND THE TWO SHALL BECOME ONE FLESH'? Mat 19:5 (Gen.2.24)

"But from the beginning of creation, God MADE THEM MALE AND FEMALE. Mar 10:6 (Gen.5.2)

"…from the blood of Abel to the blood of Zechariah, who was killed between the altar and the house of God; yes, I tell you, it shall be charged against this generation.' Luk 11:51 (Gen.4.4)

"…but on the day that Lot went out from Sodom it rained fire and brimstone from heaven and destroyed them all. Luk 17:29 (Gen.18.16-19.29)

As you read this book on "Beginnings," my goal is to help you understand God's sovereign choices, and how God superintends history and the lives of men to ac-complish His purposes. This will be a 'big picture' book to explain "why" and "how" God's works. We need the perspective of Genesis to

> *"If Jesus Christ accepted the book of Genesis as authentic, then we must also accept it as authentic.*

help us understand the remainder of the Bible correctly.

If we miss God's sovereign working in Genesis, then we will have a difficult time understanding the rest of Scripture. Remember that the Bible is a history book— 'His Story.' From Genesis to Revelation God reveals His sovereign plan step by step, so that we can see His hand working through the lives of men, women, believers, unbelievers, and nations to accomplish His plan. It involves us— but it is not really about us; it is about God, His plan, His goals, and His glory.

I will not cover all the details in Genesis, but rather I will show why God put Genesis together the way He did; and why God included the stories about some people and left out many other stories. God begins in Genesis a story that spans the entire Bible—

the story of redemption. He includes those people and events that shape and direct His plan to bring His Son— Jesus Christ, to the cross to pay the price God demands to redeem His elect.

That plan encompasses centuries of time, numerous people, many nations, and a sovereign God superintending events to accomplish His will. Through it all, God works out His story, in His way, in His timing. Let me lead you through this foundational book that starts the remarkable story of beginnings, creation, man's fall, and God's plan of redemption.

This is the first book in a series of 10 books that cover the story of the Bible. Books nine and ten are both theological novels that are available on Amazon as print books or as a Kindle ebook.[1]

---

[1] Vol. 9 is "The Story of Salvation," and vol.10 is "EPILOGUE: The Consummation of God's Eternal Plan," a novel on the book about Revelation. Both books use my pen name "Pastor John Davis"

CHAPTER 1

"CREATION"

(Genesis 1-3)

The words "In the beginning God..." elicit two different answers for the questions, "How did we get here?" or "Where did we come from?" Evolution is one answer and has many adherents and many varieties. The other answer says "God created all things..." and also has many varieties. Evolution is supported by about 87% of all US scientists according to a 2009 Pew Research poll,[2] and by 60% of the general public according to a 2013 Pew poll.[3] That same poll said 33% reject evolution. It is not my intent to answer all the arguments on either side, but rather to provide an overview of how to approach the issues.

PRELIMINARY MATTERS

Since this book is about Genesis and I hold to a creationist viewpoint, the evidence will be against evolution. However, I will not examine the evidence for or against evolution *per se*, but rather, I will give a "big picture" perspective about the two systems of thought. Once you understand the major differences and the founda-

---

[2] "Evolution, Climate Change and Other Issues". Pew Research. 2009-07-09. Retrieved 2013-03-06.

[3] www.pewforum.org/2013/12/30/publics-views-on-human-evolution/ (Dec. 30,2013)

tions of the two systems, you can then understand how the evidence is used. The first issue involves the way we think.

THE CASE ABOUT PRESUPPOSITIONS

All thinking is based on presuppositions. A presupposition is either something you assume to be true, but don't prove, or something you start with as truth, but you don't or can't prove. Let me illustrate. We all know that if you drop a glass cup on a tile floor in your kitchen, the chances are good that the cup will break.

We don't stop and evaluate Newton's law of universal gravitation that states "…every point mass in the universe attracts every other point mass with a force that is directly proportional to the product of their masses and inversely proportional to the product of

Understanding Presuppositions

Definition: "The act of presupposing; a supposition made prior to having knowledge (as for the purpose of argument)" (Advanced English Dictionary and Thesaurus, "Presupposition")

Evolution's presupposition:

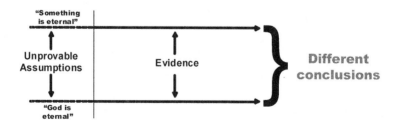

Creationism's presupposition:

Figure 1

their masses and inversely proportional to the square of the distance between them."[4] Instead, we throw up our hands in despair because one of our cups has just broken! Our presupposition is that gravity is true. We don't prove it; we just know it because of repeated examples of falling objects.

Both evolution and creationism have presuppositions. Unfortunately everyone debates the scientific evidence for and against the systems, but many fail to realize that the battle cannot be won on either side through discussion of the evidence alone. Both sides evaluate the same evidence but draw different conclusions. Why?

The battle is won or lost when we evaluate the presuppositions behind both systems. That is where I will concentrate my discussion. Having said previously that the batle is not about the evidence, please understand that the work of scientists, those who are Christians, demonstrating that science is compatible with creation is very important and must be done. The work by such organizations as the Institute for Creation Research is not only important, but necessary.[5]

THE CASE AGAINST EVOLUTION

Evolution has three major problems from my viewpoint. These issues involve their presuppositions, the simplicity of their explanations, and their attempt to use their academic credentials as leverage to prove their points

---

[4] http://en.wikipedia.org/wiki/Newton%27s _law_of_universal _gravitation

[5] ICR P.O. Box 59029, Dallas, TX 75229 (www,icr.org)

Two inadequate presuppositions

First, evolution assumes that something eternal exists without any answers about how that first "something" was able to evolve into what exists in the universe today. The first presupposition of evolution is that 'something' is eternal. Merely ask yourself this question, "Where did the first '_____' come from?"

Fill in the blank with whatever you wish to call it, and unless you are willing to say that it always existed, then something must have come before it. Push back, back, back, and eventually there will be something that always existed. Otherwise, if nothing existed, whether inanimate matter or energy, where did everything come from?

Problems with evolution

1. Evolution has an inadequate "first cause"
2. Evolution is too simple to explain our complex universe
3. Evolution scientists become philosophers to explain beginnings

Figure 2

Presuppositions applied to scientific data result in different conclusions. Let me illustrate from my personal experience. One Christmas vacation during my college years, I had the opportunity to work for several weeks with a teacher who joined our custodial staff so he could earn some extra money. We talked while we worked together and soon our subject turned to the subject of evolution. As a Bible college student I believed in creation, while he believed in evolution. Our conversation eventually turned to the subject of "Where did we come from, and how do you know it?" I kept asking "What was before that…" until one day he finally admitted that matter had to be eternal. We could then talk about our different starting points and evaluate them.

A second foundational presupposition of evolution is that *somehow,* the 'something' that is eternal, inanimate matter or some type of energy (?), begins to transform itself to eventually form what is now the universe. Unfortunately for evolution, that 'something' existed by itself alone. This raises the questions, "Was there an outside force that caused the change?" or "How did the 'something' by itself start to change?" Those questions have no adequate answers, but any proposed answer will point to "something" that exists prior to their previous starting point!

Evolution is too simple a solution for our complex world

The second fundament problem with evolution is that it is too simple an answer to explain the intricacies of the universe. The more science and technology progress, the more we understand that the universe is extremely complex. Evolution is much too simple an explanation to suggest that somehow, over millions of years, without outside manipulation, 'something' developed into the complex world we live in, or the complex unity called a human being who is so different in ability from any other creature in the universe. It takes more faith to believe evolution could develop the earth and human

27

beings than to believe in a God who created it all. Let me expand these two areas with two illustrations.

I recently watched a video on TED [6] about a new technological development in ultrasound photography that not only eliminates the surrounding tissue, but shows the fetus in vivid color. From the journey of the sperm to fertilize the egg to the birth of the baby, this video shows the development of the fetus in its various stages, forever ending the argument that eons of time could have somehow developed this amazing being.

The miracle of human birth, starts with the union of sperm and egg, develops through the marvels of DNA programming through successive stages according to a plan so intricate that it is impossible to mathematically calculate all the instructions necessary to result in birth. This amazing development results in a human being with such complex mechanisms that we still do not fully understand how the body functions.

As I watched the video and listened to the man who developed the computer program[7] explain the process of development from embryo to human being, I marveled at his inability to know how to explain the process. He used words like "unbelievable," "magic," "incredible," "marvel," until he finally said, "...the complexity of the mathematical models of how these things are done are

---

[6] http://www.youtube.com/watch?v=fKyljukBE70 Alexander Tsiaras: Conception to birth -- visualized

[7] Alexander Tsiaras

beyond human comprehension... it's a mystery, it's magic, it's divinity."[8] Such is the marvel of the human body.

The earth we live on is also so complex that evolution cannot begin to explain how such precise elements required to sustain life could happen through random chance. I'll summarize several points made by Stuart E. Nevins of the Institute for Creation Research in an article he wrote for "Acts and Facts"[9] to demonstrate that evolution is too simple an answer to explain the complexity of the earth.

- Nevins cites that the distance of the sun from the earth makes life possible. A few million miles closer or farther would end life on earth.
- The earth's tilt and rotation are so precise that a small difference in either the tilt or the length of rotation would also make life impossible.
- Another important element is the composition of the earth's atmosphere with its precise balance of chemicals that permits life to exist.
- Nevins also cites the fact that the solvency and heat capturing and holding characteristics of the atmosphere make life possible. No other planet has water to sustain life.
- Even the earth's crust has a delicate balance that keeps the oceans in place.

Together these different elements make life on earth possible; any change in any one of them would end life as we know it, yet evolution cannot explain how these "happened" to develop in

---

[8] quoted in the video http://www.youtube.com/watch_popup ?v=fKyljukBE70 Alexander Tsiaras: Conception to birth -- visualized

[9] Stuart E. Nevins has B.S. and M.S. degrees in geology, and at time of publication was Assistant Professor of Geology at Christian Heritage College. . 1974. Planet Earth: Plan or Accident? *Acts & Facts*. 3 (5).

just the right proportions, and at just the right time, in just the right sequence, to make life possible on our planet. Why do we not see this balance on other planets?

Scientists become "philosophers" when they address the issue of origins

That brings me to the third major problem in science. Proponents of evolution cease being scientists when they promote the theory of evolution, and instead become philosophers and "evolution preachers" as they extrapolate conclusions not based on science, but on their own philosophical assumptions and biases. Science by definition can only observe and experiment and draw conclusions based on what is repeatable. When a scientist draws

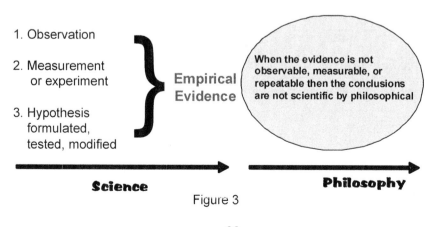

Science and Philosophy

The Scientific Method

The Oxford English Dictionary defines the scientific method as: "a method or procedure that has characterized natural science since the 17th century, consisting in systematic observation, measurement, and experiment, and the formulation, testing, and modification of hypotheses.." (Oxford English Dictionary, entry for 'Scientific Method.'

1. Observation

2. Measurement
   or experiment

3. Hypothesis
   formulated,
   tested, modified

Empirical Evidence

When the evidence is not observable, measurable, or repeatable then the conclusions are not scientific by philosophical

Science

Philosophy

Figure 3

conclusions from observations that cannot be repeated, then he moves into the area of philosophy or theology, and his assumptions determine the conclusions he makes. He has moved from the role of scientist to the role of philosopher.

Let me illustrate from the conception to birth illustration I used previously. Because the fetus looks like a tadpole at the beginning of its development in the womb, science concludes this demonstrates a leftover sequence of evolutionary development from simpler forms of life. The assumption is that similar development demonstrates the same beginning or process of development.

Now apply that same thinking to water and ice. Most liquids grow heavier as they freeze. Using the scientist's argument that similar development must result is similar conclusions, we would have to conclude that water also grows heavier as it freezes. But that conclusion is false. Water gets *lighter* as it freezes. This is a most unusual phenomenon. "One of water's many strange properties is that its solid state is less dense than its liquid state. With most compounds, it is the other way around." [10]

This unusual property makes life possible in rivers, streams, and ponds that don't freeze from the bottom up. If they did, then aquatic life would die. Therefore, just because there are similarities does not mean there is either a common source or common development. Yet most people accept what scientists say because they fail to examine the scientist's philosophical conclusions.

---

[10] http://www.evolutionnews.org/2012/08/ the_peculiar_pr_
1062861.html

The findings of science can be formulated into different philosophies, but merely being a scientist doesn't give extra credence to their philosophical conclusions, any more than being a medical doctor gives extra credence to any philosophical conclusions he might make about evolution or creation.

Yet much of the evidence for evolution is assumed to be correct because so many scientists agree with it! To that I politely say, "Baloney!" 1000 theologians, scientists, or doctors who agree upon something doesn't make it true. It only means that there are 1000 theologians, scientists or doctors who agree, but may be wrong. Truth is not found by counting bodies. Yet when you read articles about evolution, they often cite how many different scientists hold the position as though that ends the argument.

THE CASE FOR CREATION

My starting point, or presupposition, for believing in the creation of the world by God is that the Bible is a revelation from God to man. I accept this by "faith," but it is not "blind faith" as many would suggest. There is abundant evidence of the veracity of Scripture, and while it is not my objective in this chapter to evaluate all the evidence, let me at least suggest some reasons for accepting Scripture as true and authoritative. [11]

Two systems based on "faith"

Evolution starts with the presupposition that matter, or energy, or 'something' existed at the beginning. It doesn't matter what

[11] For specific evidences, read Josh McDowell's book Evidence that Demands a Verdict,

Understanding Presuppositions and Faith

Evolution's presuppositions are accepted by "faith"

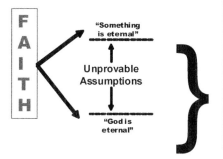

Because both starting points are unprovable, they are both accepted by "faith." The evidence alone can determine which is the better starting point

Creationism's presuppositions are accepted by "faith'

Figure 4

scientists may call it, but 'something' existed. This is accepted by "faith" since it cannot be proven. Creationism, on the other hand, also starts with a presupposition that cannot be proven. That assumption, also based on "faith," is the eternal existence of a personal Creator God. The difference between the two starting points is that the 'something' of evolution is inanimate, while the God of Creation is personal and active. Therein lies the major difference. The question for evolution is, "How does an inanimate "something" change and develop if that is all that exists?"

Which do you think is easier to accept 'by faith'—a personal being creating, or an inanimate 'something' which "somehow" develops all that now exists.

The veracity of Scripture is based on evidence- not 'blind' faith!

The Bible is a book about history and is rooted in history. Over the centuries many of the best minds have attacked the Bible seeking evidence to "prove" that the Bible is inaccurate in matters of history and science. Yet through all those years of attack, not one of those attacks has ever proven the Bible wrong or inaccurate.

Second, archaeology continues to find artifacts that demonstrate the existence of Biblical places, persons, and events. "More than 50 Old Testament and about 27 New Testament characters are known from sources other than the Bible. Of these, archaeologists have discovered the likenesses of nearly 20."[12]

The likenesses include King Shishak of Egypt (1 Kgs 14.25,26), King Jehu of Israel (2 Kgs.9.1-10.36), King Sennacherib of Assyria (2 Kgs.18.13-19.37) and King Darius I of Persia (Ezra 4.24-6.15, Hag.1.1,15). The article cited also identifies various structures that have been found that are mentioned in the Bible. Each year the spade continues to uncover evidences of the truthfulness of Scripture .

Third, the prophecies of Scripture, often written hundreds of years before the event, prove the divine nature of Scripture. Dr. Hugh Ross wrote an article in 2003 titled "Fulfilled Prophecy: Evidence for the Reliability of the Bible" that identifies a number of fulfilled prophecies. He includes a mathematical calculation of the probability of 'chance' fulfillment. I'll include just three of his

[12]   http://www.bibleuniverse.com/articles/bible-universe-blog/articletype /articleview/articleid/ 1584/pageid/1718.aspx

examples of the wide variety of evidences that fulfilled prophecy encompasses. Notice in the footnotes the numbers for the possibility of chance fulfillment of the prophecies.

> "In approximately 700 B.C. the prophet Micah named the tiny village of Bethlehem as the birthplace of Israel's Messiah (Micah 5:2). The fulfillment of this prophecy in the birth of Christ is one of the most widely known and widely celebrated facts in history. (Probability of chance fulfillment = 1 in 10^5.)" [13]

> "Some 400 years before crucifixion was invented, both Israel's King David and the prophet Zechariah described the Messiah's death in words that perfectly depict that mode of execution. Further, they said that the body would be pierced and that none of the bones would be broken, contrary to customary procedure in cases of crucifixion (Psalm 22 and 34:20; Zechariah 12:10). Again, historians and New Testament writers confirm the fulfillment: Jesus of Nazareth died on a Roman cross, and his extraordinarily quick death eliminated the need for the usual breaking of bones. A spear was thrust into his side to verify that he was, indeed, dead. (Probability of chance fulfillment = 1 in 10^{13}.)" [14]

> "Joshua prophesied that Jericho would be rebuilt by one man. He also said that the man's eldest son would die when the reconstruction began and that his youngest son would die when the work reached completion (Joshua 6:26). About five centuries later this prophecy found its fulfillment in the life and family of a man named Hiel (1 Kings 16:33-34). (Probability of chance fulfillment = 1 in 10^7)." [15]

The Bible stands undaunted in spite of all the attacks and its many detractors. God gives ample evidence in Scripture regarding both how He created and why He created.

THE GENESIS RECORD ON GOD'S METHODS

There are different ideas among creationists about the Genesis record. Some want to reconcile the Bible with science and see

---

[13] Ibid (or 1 in 1,00,000)

[14] Ibid (or 1 in 10,000,000,000,000)

[15] Ibid (or 1 in 10,000,000)

"long days" in Genesis 1. Others like the "Big Bang" theory where God started creation and evolution continued it. However, let me be very clear. We do not need to reconcile science and the Bible! They don't contradict each other, nor are they incompatible! It is only when we accept the presuppositions of evolution that we believe we must reconcile the Bible with science. But science fits perfectly with the record of Genesis if we ignore evolutionary presuppositions.

The work of ICR is just one of many good organizations demonstrating that science and the Bible are completely compatible.[16] The following observations from the Genesis record detail the methods God used in creation.

The Biblical record in Genesis tells us about God's creative activity and the rest of Scripture supports that description and clarifies it. Scriptures writers in the other books of the Bible do not attempt to "prove" the Genesis record, they assume its truthfulness as they relate material about God and His work. I'll discuss the following points:

1. Ex Nihilo
2. Instantaneously
3. In an orderly way
4. In 6 24 hour days
5. Fully mature

EX NIHILO

Ex nihilo is Latin for "from nothing."[17] This concept is not limited to

---

[16] ICR publishes an excellent free magazine "Acts and Facts" which explains scientific issues from a creation viewpoint.

[17] http://www.merriam-webster.com/dictionary/ex%20nihilo or http://www.thefreedictionary.com /ex I nihilo

creationism alone! Henry Morris[18], cites physicist Edward P. Tryon, an evolutionist as one of the first to propound this idea.

In 1973, I proposed that our Universe had been created spontaneously from nothing (ex nihilo), as a result of established principles of physics. This proposal variously struck people as preposterous, enchanting, or both."[19]

So while many try to say that creating out of nothing is an invalid assumption, evolution scientists accept the possibility of the idea. Genesis clearly attributes creation to God who created all things "out of nothing."

Gen 1:1- In the beginning, God created the heavens and the earth.

Several important observations should be made. First, God's creative activity marks the 'beginning' of all things spatial. Before God created there was God— only God. Time began when God created. Second, God is distinct from His creation and He transcends His creation, meaning that God transcends time and space. His infinity and eternality are concepts too difficult for finite minds to comprehend, yet according to Genesis 1.1 they are true.

---

[18] Dr. Morris (1918-2006), PhD, was Founder of the Institute for Creation Research.

[19] Tryon, E. P. 1984. What Made the World? New Scientist. 101: 14. Cited in Morris, H. 2011. Evolution Ex Nihilo. Acts & Facts. 40 (9): 4-5.

Third, the Hebrew term 'bara' is used 55[20] times in Scripture and is limited to God's creative activity in 52 of the 55 references. Only Josh.17.15, Ezk.21.19, 23.47 use the term 'bara' apart from God as the subject. This term is translated in the NASB by "brings about (1), clear (2), create (6), created (32), creates (1), creating (3), Creator (4), cut them down (1), make (2), produced (1)." [21]

Other passages of Scripture reinforce this concept that God created all that exists 'out of nothing.'

> Rom 4:17- (as it is written, "A FATHER OF MANY NATIONS HAVE I MADE YOU") in the presence of Him whom he believed, even God, who gives life to the dead and calls into being that which does not exist.

> Col 1:16- For by Him all things were created, both in the heavens and on earth, visible and invisible, whether thrones or dominions or rulers or authorities--all things have been created through Him and for Him.

> Heb 11:3- By faith we understand that the worlds were prepared by the word of God, so that what is seen was not made out of things which are visible.

That God created out of nothing is no more difficult to accept than the scientist who says that "something" inanimate eternally existed and "somehow" began to change over eons of time so that it results in what now exists.

INSTANTANEOUSLY

When God created, He spoke, and things happened. God created instantaneously and Scriptures outside of Genesis supports

---

[20] See endnote # 1 at the end of the book for a list of references.

[21] e-sword NASEC lexicon, H1254a

Instantaneous Creation

1. "**God said**..."   - 3,6,9,11,14,20,24,26,28 and 29.

2. "...**and it was so**"   - 7, 9,11,15,24,30

3. "...**there was**..."   - 3,5,8,13,19,23,31

4. "**God saw**..."   - 4,10,12,18,21,25,31

5. Then follows a **creative act** of God

a. "Separated"	– light/darkness	
	– **day 1** – (1.3-6)	
b. "Made" and separated"	– expanse between waters above/below	
	– **day 2** – (1.7,8)	
c. "Let be gathered..."	– waters below	
"Let the earth sprout..."	– vegetation, plants, fruit trees	
	– **day 3** (1.9-13)	
d. "Made and placed"	– sun/ moon	
	– **day 4** – (1.14-19)	
e. "God created"	– God blessed" - sea monsters, fish, birds	
	– be fruitful/multiply	
	– **day 5** – (1.20-23)	
f. "God made"	– beasts, cattle, creeping things	
g. "God created"	– man	
"God gave"	– plants, fruit	
	– **day 6** – (1.24-30)	

6. "**God called**..."   –1.5,8,10

---

that truth. Notice the different words that refer to God speaking things into existence.

> Psa 33:6- By the *word* of the LORD the heavens were made, And by the breath of His mouth all their host.

> Psa 148:5- Let them praise the name of the LORD, For He *commanded* and they were created.

Notice the repeated formulas in Genesis 1 on the chart below that emphasize immediate creation---- "God said," "and it was so," "there was," and "God saw."

IN AN ORDERLY WAY

God does not give precise details about "how" He did His work of creating, but from the record of Scripture we get glimpses that God's creative activity was orderly. Different words describe this activity. Scripture says God "made" the sea, and "formed" the dry land" (Ps.95.5). God "made" and "formed" man (Is.2916). God "formed" light and "created" darkness (Is.45.7). God "stretched out" the heavens (Is.42.5, 45.12, 51.13). God "laid" the foundations of the earth (Is.51.13, Heb.1.10). God "created" the stars and "calls them by name" (Is.40.6).

These are just a few of the descriptions that tell us that God's work of creating was orderly. That brings us to the major conflict among those who believe in creationism. "How long did creation take?"

IN SIX 24-HOUR DAYS

I believe that God created in six literal 24-hour days. The only reason to seek for some other time frame for the "days" of Genesis is an attempt to reconcile evolutionary presuppositions that say the earth is millions or maybe billions of years old. Remember this truth: "If you start out going in the wrong direction, you will never arrive at your destination." Evolution has no explanation for "when" or "how" things came to be, so they assume an inadequate starting point and add "time" to try to make their answers plausible.

There are many good books and articles that address the use of the Hebrew word "yom"[22] (day), so I'll limit my comments to an overview of the issue.

The word "Yom" is used 2267 times in the Old Testament as Figure 6 indicates. Moses uses "Yom" 655 times in the Pentateuch and 147 of those times "Yom" is used in Genesis. I'll summarize the major arguments for a six day creation of 24-hour days.

The Use of "YOM" (Day)

1. In the Pentateuch	-	655
Genesis	-	147
Exodus	-	113
Leviticus	-	109
Numbers	-	118
2. In the rest of the Old Testament		- 1612
		2267

Figure 6

1. "Yom" always refers to a 24-hour when used with a number outside Genesis.[23] Stambaugh says "Yom" with a number occurs 357 times outside Genesis and because it always refers to a 24 hour day, he therefore concludes it must mean the same in Genesis. An example is Ex.24.16.

> Exodus 24:16: "And the glory of the Lord abode upon Mount Sinai, and the cloud covered it six days, and on the seventh day He called unto Moses out of the midst of the cloud."

2. The phrase "evening and morning" occurs at least 20 times in the Old Testament and refers to a literal 24-hour day. Here are several examples from Exodus.

---

[22] See endnote # 2 for books and articles on "Yom" e-sword NASEC lexicon, H1254a

[23] James Stambaugh, http://www.icr.org/article/288/ (Mr. Stambaugh is Librarian at the Institute for Creation Research)

Exo 16:8- Moses said, "This will happen when the LORD gives you meat to eat in the evening, and bread to the full in the morning; for the LORD hears your grumblings which you grumble against Him. And what are we? Your grumblings are not against us but against the LORD."

Exo 27:21- "In the tent of meeting, outside the veil which is before the testimony, Aaron and his sons shall keep it in order from evening to morning before the LORD; it shall be a perpetual statute throughout their generations for the sons of Israel.

3. John Whitcomb gives the following argument from 2 Peter 3 regarding the six 24-hour literal days.

"The 'day' of 2 Peter 3:8 must be a literal day in order for the contrast with 'a thousand years' to be protected. God can do in a

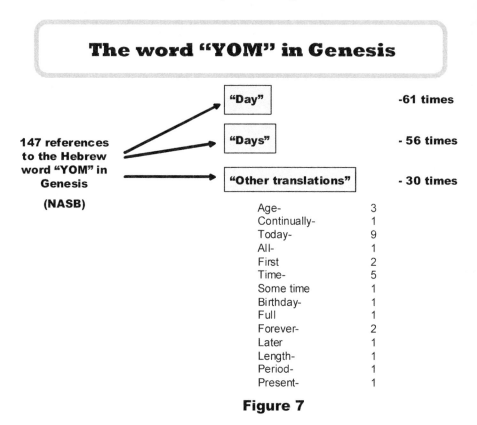

Figure 7

very short time what men or "nature" would require a very long time (if ever) to accomplish. This is why sinful mankind would naturally prefer to stretch God's days of creation to cover vast periods of time.[24]

This concurs with the argument that the Hebrew word "Yom" when used with a number always refers to a 24-hour day. Numbers become meaningless when used with "Yom" or in reference to the idea of a 24-hour day if "day" refers to a long period of time. Whitcomb makes this point when he says "The "days" of Genesis 1:14 must be literal or the word "years" in the same verse would be meaningless."[25]

4. Liberal Hebrew professors who do not believe in Genesis as history still understand "day" as a literal 24-hour day. Ken Ham quotes Dr. James Barr, Regius Professor of Hebrew at Oxford University, who makes the following statement.

> "So far as I know, there is no professor of Hebrew or Old Testament at any world-class university who does not believe that the writer(s) of Gen. 1–11 intended to convey to their readers the ideas that (a) creation took place in a series of six days which were the same as the days of 24 hours we now experience (b) the figures contained in the Genesis genealogies provided by simple addition a chronology from the beginning of the world up to later stages in the biblical story (c) Noah's Flood was understood to be worldwide and extinguish all human and animal life except for those in the ark."[26]

In the same article Ken Ham cites professor Marcus Dods, New College, Edinburgh who says,

---

[24] http://www.rae.org/pdf/dayfaq.pdf, quoting from his book The Bible and Astronomy pp.21-22:

[25] Ibid

[26] http://www.answersingenesis.org/articles/nab/could-god-have-created-in-six-days

"If, for example, the word "day" in these chapters does not mean a period of twenty-four hours, the interpretation of Scripture is hopeless."[27]

The God who wrote the Bible used the word "Yom" to communicate that He created in six literal 24-hour days. The only reason for seeking some other time reference is an attempt to reconcile science with Scripture. As we have demonstrated, science will never be able to answer the question of origins— that is a question for philosophers and theologians to wrestle with.

FULLY MATURE

One of the common objections to creation in six days is that the earth appears to be very old, several billion years old, depending upon which scientist you read. We don't accept the objections of evolution because of their wrong presuppositions, but there is a simple answer to the issue: God created the earth in a mature state when He created it. This is not a problem for a God who created all that exists. The Genesis record indicates vegetation that produced fruit with "seed in them" on day two, birds that flew on day five, and a mature man and woman on day six, and animals and man who could "...be fruitful and multiply." There was no evolutionary development. Mat 19:4 says,

> And He answered and said, "Have you not read that He who created them from the beginning MADE THEM MALE AND FE-MALE,

The other side of the answer says that the way scientists date things is based upon their presuppositions of evolutionary develop-

---

[27] Ibid

ment. For instance, a scientist will date a certain rock as thousands or millions of years old because of the strata or level it is found in. Therefore anything found in that strata is of the same age. However, in other areas of the world, this same rock in a different strata is dated the same age, even though the strata is different!

God can do whatever He chooses to do. He could have chosen another way to create the universe, but He didn't. Since God wrote the Scripture, He tells us how He created. The only reasons for not believing what the Bible says is 1) not believing God exists; or 2) trying to correlate scientific data with Scripture. Those who refuse to believe the Biblical account of creation are left without an explanation of who we are, how we got here, and what happens to us when we die. Those who want to reconcile the Bible with science are left with the dilemma of accepting the unproven and inadequate presuppositions of science and rejecting the truthfulness of Scripture. Both positions cannot be correct since they contradict one anther.

In review

Both scientists and Christians develops their models for the universe based on presuppositions. The starting points are equal. The question is: "Which model best fits the facts?" Science adds time whenever it can't answer issues, and changes its model to fit new facts; the Bible account of creation remains unchanged and has never been proven inaccurate in spite of new scientific discoveries. In fact, time after time the Bible account of creation has been proven accurate. Archaeology and scientific experiments demonstrate the veracity of Scripture. Unfortunately, scientists rarely admit they are wrong, they just change their theory to accommodate the evidence. Technology has increased man's ability to explore the universe, study the body, examine data more quickly, yet there are neither proofs the Bible is wrong, nor evidence that evolution is on the right track as an answer.

God created, in six literal 24-hour days, out of nothing, everything that exists. The reason men and women turn to evolution is that they do not want to admit there is a Creator who gives moral directives, and has declared that man is separated from Him because of sin and needs a savior: Jesus Christ. That is the dilemma that causes men to turn to evolution.

CHAPTER 2

CORRUPTION

(Genesis 3, Romans 5, Galatians 5, Ephesians 2)

God created Adam and Eve and placed them in a perfect environment. God specifically created the Garden of Eden for Adam and Eve. Genesis 2.8-10 says,

> "The LORD God planted a garden toward the east, in Eden; and there He placed the man whom He had formed. Out of the ground the LORD God caused to grow every tree that is pleasing to the sight and good for food; the tree of life also in the midst of the garden, and the tree of the knowledge of good and evil. Now a river flowed out of Eden to water the garden; and from there it divided and became four rivers."

The word "planted" means "to plant, fasten, fix, establish"[28] Apparently this garden was especially designed to test whether Adam and Eve would obey God or not. God provided for their every need and God's instructions were clear.

> "Then the LORD God took the man and put him into the garden of Eden to cultivate it and keep it. The LORD God commanded the man, saying, "From any tree of the garden you may eat freely; but from the tree of the knowledge of good and evil you shall not eat, for in the day that you eat from it you will surely die." (Gen 2:15-17)

These verses reveal several significant truths.

1. God placed Adam in the garden on the sixth day of creation
2. God gave specific instructions to Adam
    a. You may eat from any tree but one
    b. You may not eat from the tree of the knowledge of good and evil

---

[28] Brown, Driver, Briggs lexicon in e-sword (BDB)

   c. If you eat of the forbidden tree you will die
     that day
  3. Eve was not yet created when God gave Adam the in
     structions

On the sixth day Adam named all the animals, but because God saw that man did not have a mate, God created Eve from Adam's rib that same day. We do not know how long Adam and Eve lived in the garden before the events of chapter 3, but paradise was about to be corrupted. The story of Genesis 3 changed the course of human history forever.

THE TEMPTATION OF SATAN

Satan's original name was Lucifer [29] which means "the morning star." While this passage speaks specifically about the king of Babylon, or the king of Tyre in Ezekiel 28.12, the reference goes beyond a description for an earthly king and applies to Satan.[30] We learn a number of important truths about Lucifer from Ezekiel 28.

  1. He is a created being (28.13)
  2. He was perfect in wisdom and beauty (28.12)
  3. He was in Eden (28.13)
  4. He was in an exalted position in God's economy
     (28.14) [31]
  5. He guarded God's throne (28.14) [32]

---

[29] Is.14.12 "the *morning star:* - Lucifer." So translated in the KJV

[30] See Ezk.28.12-17 and Rev.12.10-12 for additional references

[31] "Anointed" is from a Hebrew root which means 'to expand' Brown, Driver, Briggs lexicon in e-sword (BDB)

[32] The Hebrew word means to "to *fence* in, *cover* over, (figuratively) *protect:* - cover, defense, *(sic)* defend, hedge in, join together, set, shut up." (BDB)

6.   He was blameless until some unrighteousness occurred (28.15)

7.   His beauty caused pride to develop (28.17)

Lucifer was cast from heaven with 1/3 of the angels [33] and given control of the earth. This occurred sometime between Genesis 1.31 and Genesis 3.1 [34] Satan is called "the prince of the power of the air" and the "spirit that is now working in the sons of disobedience." [35] Genesis 3 says Satan used a serpent [36] "who was more cunning than any beast of the field which the Lord had made." [37] However, Paul says that Satan also "...disguises himself as an angel of light." [38]

Satan approached Eve alone in the Garden as a serpent. This is the first time in Scripture that a human being speaks to an animal. The other time Balaam spoke to his rebellious donkey.[39] It is interesting that neither Eve nor Balaam expressed surprise in the situation. Satan's attack is bold and successful.

QUESTION: "designed to instill doubt about truth"

---

[33] Rev.12.4

[34] God called everything "very good" in Genesis 1.31, "...God saw all that He had made, and behold, it was very good."

[35] Eph.2.2

[36] Note while the word means 'snake,' this is not a snake as we know them today. It apparently walked upright.

[37] Gen.3.1

[38] 2 Cor.11.14

[39] Num.22.28,28. We know that God opened the donkey's mouth so he could speak to Balaam, but whether or not the serpent in Genesis 3 could speak or was empowered by Satan is unknown. That Eve was not surprised when the serpent spoke does not necessarily indicate serpents could talk. There is no indication that God's curse involved the cessation of speech.

Satan framed the question in a negative fashion. "Has God said, "You shall not eat from any tree of the garden?" The addition of the word "Indeed" makes this a challenge to God's authority and to Eve's "rights" as a free person to determine her own way. The expected answer from Eve should have been an emphatic "No," followed by an accurate statement of God's command. While Eve did respond with a partial restatement of God's command she did not respond to the challenge to God's authority and also added the words "…or touch it…" which were not part of God's command to Adam. [40] Satan quickly moved from a question to a bold statement.

STATEMENT: "Designed to instill doubt about God's truthfulness"

Satan did not address Eve's addition but immediately made a bold statement—" You surely will not die!" [41] Remember that Satan is cunning and his method is designed to cause Eve to doubt God's truthfulness. Satan did not allow Eve to respond, but immediately began to explain why his statement was true! He wanted Eve to accept his word and ignore God's word. This is always Satan's attack. "Believe me rather than God."

---

[40] Gen.3.3. Why Eve added this part is unclear. It may have been either something Adam told her so she wouldn't go near the tree, or it might have been a response indicating she felt God's instructions were too harsh.

[41] Gen.3.4

EXPLANATION: "Designed to illicit agreement"

Satan boldly explains that God has kept important information from them. "For God knows…" begins Satan's greatest deception. He tells Eve a partial truth, and minimizes the consequences that result from disobeying God. It is true that Adam and Eve would know good and evil, but Satan doesn't tell Eve that the knowledge would not be merely intellectual, but experiential! Satan also diverts Eve attention from the consequence of death that God promised Adam if he ate the fruit.

Satan's greatest scheme is first to get humans to concentrate on what they are missing, and second to conceal the consequences of their choices. If we see how good it is, then we want it so much that the consequences seem unimportant in comparison to the benefit of what we desire.

SUCCESS OF THE TEMPTATION

Eve saw that the tree was good for food. She saw that it was beautiful. She believed Satan's lie that it would make her wise, so she took of the fruit and gave some to Adam who ate it. Paradise was lost when Adam chose to eat of the fruit of the tree of the knowledge of good and evil that Eve offered to him. The Scripture is very clear that Eve was deceived, but Adam made a deliberate choice to eat of the fruit.[42]

"And it was not Adam who was deceived, but the woman being deceived, fell into transgression." (1Ti 2:14)

_____

[42] We are not told what God would have done if Adam had refused to eat of the fruit. Eve's deception did not excuse her sin, and whether God would have provided a cleansing for her is beyond the scope of our information.

The Scriptures are also very clear that it was Adam's sin, as the head of the race, who brought God's judgment upon the entire human race. Adam was our representative; his choice became our choice; and his curse became our curse. This is clear in a number of Biblical references.

> Therefore, just as through one man sin entered into the world, and death through sin, and so death spread to all men, because all sinned—" (Rom 5:12)

> For since by a man came death, by a man also came the resurrection of the dead. (1Co 15:21)

We do not like this truth because we think we are autonomous, a free person, with the right to choose our own way. Indeed we have done exactly that according to Is.53.6.

> "All of us like sheep have gone astray, Each of us has turned to his own way; But the LORD has caused the iniquity of us all To fall on Him."

Unfortunately, our own way is the way of sin. We sin because we are sinners— that is our nature. We are not sinners because we sin. This is such an important distinction that 1 John 1.8-10 states it very clearly.

> "If we say that we have no sin, we are deceiving ourselves and the truth is not in us. If we confess our sins, He is faithful and righteous to forgive us our sins and to cleanse us from all unrighteousness. If we say that we have not sinned, we make Him a liar and His word is not in us."

Did you catch the distinction between "we have no sin" (nature) and "we have not sinned" (acts)? That brings us to the consequences of sin for Adam and Eve and for the entire race.

THE CONSEQUENCES OF SIN

Man does not want to acknowledge that he is a sinner before God. However, the fact that every person on this planet faces death evidences the judgment of God upon the race. Adam's sin brought not only immediate consequences upon himself and Eve, but upon the entire race.

THE IMMEDIATE CONSEQUENCES FOR ADAM AND EVE

Eve bought into Satan's deception and forgot that eating the fruit would bring serious consequences. Adam, knowing the consequences, still chose to participate with Eve in rebellion against God. Immediately the consequences of sin became evident from their actions. Genesis 3.7-24 lists the consequences to Adam and Eve once their eyes were opened experientially to sin.

Immediate consequences
1. **Sin with its shame**
2. **Spiritual death**
3. **Physical death**
4. **Expulsion from the Garden**
5. **Toil, trouble and pain,**
6. **Pain in child-bearing**
7. **Difficulties in the marriage relationship**

Sin with its shame

"Then the eyes of both of them were opened, and they knew that they were naked; and they sewed fig leaves together and made themselves loin coverings. They heard the sound of the LORD God walking in the garden in the cool of the day, and the man and his wife hid themselves from the presence of the LORD God among the trees of the garden."

1.   They realized they were naked

Prior to the entrance of sin, Adam and Eve wore no clothes and were unashamed. The first consequence of sin was an understanding that they were naked. Adam and Eve bought into Satan's lie and lost their innocence. What was once a beautiful relationship now brought a sense of shame. Augustine rightly said "Sin is its own punishment."[43] Adam and Eve immediately cut fig leaves to cover their shame.

2. They hid from God

God appeared regularly to visit with Adam and Eve and when they heard His voice in the cool of the day they hid from Him among the trees of the garden. God called to Adam "Where are you?" Adam came out from among the trees and replied,

> He said, "I heard the sound of You in the garden, and I was afraid because I was naked; so I hid myself." (Gen 3:10)

Man has been hiding from God since Adam. Covering our sin is frivolous; hiding is frivolous. God knows our sin and God knows where we are. David said it so clearly in Ps.139.

> "You know when I sit down and when I rise up; You understand my thought from afar. You scrutinize my path and my lying down, And are intimately acquainted with all my ways....Where can I go from Your Spirit? Or where can I flee from Your presence? If I ascend to heaven, You are there; If I make my bed in Sheol, behold, You are there. If I take the wings of the dawn, If I dwell in the remotest part of the sea, Even there Your hand will lead me, And Your right hand will lay hold of me." (Psa 139:2,3, 7-10)

---

[43]Confessions of Saint Augustine

3. They try to excuse their sin

God now asks Adam. "Who told you that you were naked? Have you eaten from the tree of which I commanded you not to eat?" (Gen 3:11) Adam's response indicates how deeply sin affects us. He tries immediately to blame Eve. She in turn tries to blame Satan. Listen to their excuses.

> "The man said, "The woman whom You gave to be with me, she gave me from the tree, and I ate." Then the LORD God said to the woman, "What is this you have done?" And the woman said, "The serpent deceived me, and I ate." (Gen 3:12-13)

Both of their excuses were an attempt to shift blame to someone else rather that accept personal responsibility for their actions. The tendency to blame others for our sin continues to this day as the stock reply whenever sin is exposed. God did not accept their excuses, and explains the second major consequence.

Spiritual death

Spiritual death was the consequence that God said would occur when He gave Adam the prohibition of eating from the tree of the knowledge of good and evil. Spiritual death means separation from God in all its fullness. This occurred immediately when Adam and Eve sinned. It is the state of the entire human race since Genesis 3.

Spiritual death alienates man from God. Spiritual death also affects our moral nature so that being born in sin means that we are sinners from birth and morally damaged. We cannot please God and we cannot do anything "good" in God's sight.[44]

---

[44] Rom.3.10

Physical death

Physical death is the third major consequence of sin. Rom.5.12 and 1 Cor.15.22 indicate it is the penalty for all humans. Ezekiel says twice in one chapter "The soul who sins will die. "[45] The moment we are born we begin the journey to death.

Expulsion from the garden

Adam and Eve were driven out of the beautiful garden of Eden that God had made for them.

> "So He drove the man out; and at the east of the garden of Eden He stationed the cherubim and the flaming sword which turned every direction to guard the way to the tree of life." Gen 3:24

Sin always causes us to lose God's blessings. Unconfessed sin breaks a Christian's fellowship with God. That is why 1 John 1.9 is so important for the Christian.

> "If we confess our sins, He is faithful and righteous to forgive us our sins and to cleanse us from all unrighteousness."

The word "confess" means to "say the same thing"[46] When we acknowledge our sin to God, fellowship is restored. Being cast out of the Garden resulted in the next consequence of sin: hard work necessary to sustain their lives.

Toil, trouble, and pain

Life in the Garden of Eden did not require hard labor prior to the entrance of sin into the world. But once Adam sinned, God cursed the ground so that it now produced thorns and thistles. It required hard work and sweat labor to grow food to sustain life.

---

[45] Ezk.18.4,20

[46] Thayer's lexicon in e-sword

"Then to Adam He said, "Because you have listened to the voice of your wife, and have eaten from the tree about which I commanded you, saying, 'You shall not eat from it'; Cursed is the ground because of you; In toil you will eat of it All the days of your life. "Both thorns and thistles it shall grow for you; And you will eat the plants of the field; By the sweat of your face You will eat bread, Till you return to the ground, Because from it you were taken; For you are dust, And to dust you shall return." (Gen 3:17-19)

Rom 8:19-22 reminds us that the creation itself awaits the time when God will cleanse the curse of sin from the universe.

"For the anxious longing of the creation waits eagerly for the revealing of the sons of God. For the creation was subjected to futility, not willingly, but because of Him who subjected it, in hope that the creation itself also will be set free from its slavery to corruption into the freedom of the glory of the children of God. For we know that the whole creation groans and suffers the pains of childbirth together until now."

This will not happen until after the Tribulation, after the 1,000 year Millennium, after the assignment of Satan and his demons to eternal fire, and after the final judgment of unbelievers at the Great White Throne judgment. All unbelievers will be assigned forever to the Lake of fire with Satan and his demons. God will then destroy the universe down to the very atoms and recreate new heavens and earth.[47] The next consequence affects Eve and all women.

Pain in child-bearing

God says that Eve, and all women following her, will have greater pain in child-bearing.

To the woman He said, "I will greatly multiply Your pain in childbirth, In pain you will bring forth children..." (Gen 3:16)

---

[47] 2 Pet.3.7,10,12,13

Every painful childbirth is a reminder of two important truths. First, that Eve gave birth to sin through her acceptance of Satan's lies. Second, Paul reminds all women in 1 Tim.2.15 that the pain of childbirth should be a stimulus to raise godly children and thus stop the reign of sin in their children who receive Christ as Savior.

> "But women will be preserved through the bearing of children if they continue in faith and love and sanctity with self-restraint." (1Ti 2:15)

The next consequence of sin involves not only Adam and Eve, but all married couples. God says that sin will cause difficulties in their marriage relationship.

Difficulties in the marriage relationship

Wouldn't it be great to be able to go back in time and experience the marriage relationship before sin entered the world? The former harmonious pre-sin marital relationship has become a tug-of-war as two self-centered wills struggle for ascendancy.

> "...Yet your desire will be for your husband, And he will rule over you." Gen 3:16

The word "desire" in this verse is from a root that means "...stretching out after"[48] and is used in a negative sense to indicate that the woman will try to usurp the man's leadership role, but that he will "rule" over her.[49] Throughout history most marriages reflect this struggle of husbands and wives for the leadership role. God ordained that Adam be the head of the family, and while the hus-

---

[48] BDB lexicon in e-sword. Gen.3.16

[49] lexicon in e-sword- "to rule, have dominion, reign"

band's role is not related to superiority, sin causes tension as husbands over-emphasize authority and wives equate submission to inferiority.

THE CURSE UPON THE SERPENT AND SATAN

God turns from Adam and Eve to the source of the temptation. He curses both the serpent that Satan used as well as Satan himself.

The snake

Genesis 3.1 says the serpent was "more crafty than any beast of the field which the LORD God had made." In Mt.10.16. Jesus uses the cunning of snakes and doves as a methodology when he sends the disciples out to evangelize. [50] Snakes in the Garden of Eden were much different that snakes as we know them today.

Snakes may have had legs and walked upright. It is even possible they could speak since Eve was not surprised to hear the serpent speaking to her. Whatever their ability, God curses the snake as being culpable even though Satan used it. God curses the snake above all other animals and relegates it to crawling on its belly and eating dust.

Satan

Satan's curse is found in Gen.3.15,

"And I will put enmity Between you and the woman, And between your seed and her seed; He shall bruise you on the head, And you shall bruise him on the heel." (Gen 3:15)

---

[50] "Behold, I send you out as sheep in the midst of wolves; so be shrewd as serpents and innocent as doves.

While there is no change in subject from the physical serpent, God addresses Satan and says there will be enmity between
Satan's seed and the woman. Satan does not have literal 'seed'
except in the sense of human beings he controls. Jesus explains this
when He said in John 8.44,

> "You are of your father the devil, and you want to do the desires
> of your father. He was a murderer from the beginning, and does
> not stand in the truth because there is no truth in him. Whenever
> he speaks a lie, he speaks from his own nature, for he is a liar and
> the father of lies." (Joh 8:44)

Unbelievers are children of Satan. Paul continues that
thought in Ephesians 2.2 when he says,

> "And you were dead in your trespasses and sins, in which you
> formerly walked according to the course of this world, according
> to the prince of the power of the air, of the spirit that is now
> working in the sons of disobedience." (Eph 2:2)

Therefore, between those who follow Christ and those who
reject Christ there is enmity. The Gospel separates people into these
two camps. Remember Jesus said in Mt.10.34-36,

> "Do not think that I came to bring peace on the earth; I did not
> come to bring peace, but a sword. "For I came to SET A MAN
> AGAINST HIS FATHER, AND A DAUGHTER AGAINST HER
> MOTHER, AND A DAUGHTER-IN-LAW AGAINST HER MOTH-
> ER-IN-LAW; and A MAN'S ENEMIES WILL BE THE MEMBERS
> OF HIS HOUSEHOLD."

However, God identifies one of Eve's children who will
bruise Satan's head and Satan will bruise His heel. This is a reference to Christ and is the first statement of the Gospel. Christ frees
all who receive Him as Savior and Lord from Satan's control. Note
the following verses that speak of Satan's defeat and the deliverance
of the believer from his power.

"Therefore, since the children share in flesh and blood, He Himself likewise also partook of the same, that through death He might render powerless him who had the power of death, that is, the devil, and might free those who through fear of death were subject to slavery all their lives." Heb 2:14-15

"For though we walk in the flesh, we do not war according to the flesh, for the weapons of our warfare are not of the flesh, but divinely powerful for the destruction of fortresses. We are destroying speculations and every lofty thing raised up against the knowledge of God, and we are taking every thought captive to the obedience of Christ, and we are ready to punish all disobedience, whenever your obedience is complete." 2Co 10:3-6

"...the one who practices sin is of the devil; for the devil has sinned from the beginning. The Son of God appeared for this purpose, to destroy the works of the devil." 1Jn 3:8

Satan can only cause Christ suffering, but Christ destroyed Satan's works at the cross, and then one day will assign him to the Lake of Fire forever according to Rev.20.10.

"And the devil who deceived them was thrown into the lake of fire and brimstone, where the beast and the false prophet are also; and they will be tormented day and night forever and ever."

Unfortunately, not only were there immediate consequences for Adam and Eve, but there are continuing consequences for the human race because of Adam's sin.

THE CONTINUING CONSEQUENCES OF DEATH FOR THE HUMAN RACE

God said death would be the consequence for eating of the tree of the knowledge of good and evil when Adam received the instructions in Gen 2:16-17.

The LORD God commanded the man, saying, "From any tree of the garden you may eat freely; but from the tree of the knowledge of good and evil you shall not eat, for in the day that you eat from it you will surely die."

Neither Adam nor Eve died physically after eating the fruit so it would seem at first glance that the consequence was invalid. However, there are several interesting comments in Gen 3:22-24 worth noting.

> "Then the LORD God said, "Behold, the man has become like one of Us, knowing good and evil; and now, he might stretch out his hand, and take also from the tree of life, and eat, and live forever"-- therefore the LORD God sent him out from the garden of Eden, to cultivate the ground from which he was taken. So He drove the man out; and at the east of the garden of Eden He stationed the cherubim and the flaming sword which turned every direction to guard the way to the tree of life."

First, God said Adam and Eve now knew experientially about good and evil. Second, God said that man might take from the "tree of life, and eat, and live forever..." so God drove Adam and Eve from the Garden of Eden and stationed a cherubim to guard the tree of life. There are 11 references in Scripture to the "tree of life." 7 of the references refer to the tree of life like the one in Eden. The other references refer to human traits that are a tree of life. [51] God driving Adam and Eve from the Garden was an act of mercy lest they be forever lost in their state of sinfulness.[52] Three consequences, summarized by the word "death," happen to the human race.

Physical death

Physical death and its decay began to happen immediately after Adam sinned. His body began a downward cycle that for Adam

---

[51] In the Garden of Eden: Gen.2.9, 3.22,24. In heaven: Rev.2.7, 22.2,14,19. To human traits: Prov.3.18, 11.30, 13.12, 15.4.

[52] Since the tree of life was in the middle of the Garden and they could eat of it, why Adam and Eve had not eaten from it already forever remains a mystery.

lasted 930 years. But each successive generation lived shorter lives as God allowed the processes of death to invade the human body.

Death passes from parent to child by the decree of God [53] and only Enoch and Elijah escape the curse of physical death.

Those Christians living at the Rapture will also escape death as they receive their heavenly bodies immediately.[54] However, every other human being will die as a consequence of Adam's sin and their own sin. But physical death is not the only consequence. Spiritual death is the second consequence upon the human race.

Spiritual death

Spiritual death also occurred for Adam and Eve upon their eating of the tree. There are two different aspects to this conse-quence. The first aspect of spiritual death separates man from God. Adam and Eve demonstrated this when they hid from God in the Garden. Men have been hiding from God ever since. Isa 59:2 says,

> "But your iniquities have made a separation between you and your God, And your sins have hidden His face from you so that He does not hear."

Rom.3.23 reminds us that "...all have sinned and fall short of the glory of God...." and Rom.6.23 says the "the wages of sin is death." The separation results in mankind becoming God's enemies,[55] and God says we now live under His wrath.[56] We are

---

[53] Rom.5.12, I Cor.15.22

[54] 1 Cor.15.23, 1 Thess.4.16,17

[55] Rom.5.10

[56] Rom.5.9, Jn.3.18,36

born separated from God. But there is a second aspect to spiritual death.

The second aspect of spiritual death is the decay of man's moral nature. Eph.2.1-3 says,

> "And you were dead in your trespasses and sins, in which you formerly walked according to the course of this world, according to the prince of the power of the air, of the spirit that is now working in the sons of disobedience. Among them we too all formerly lived in the lusts of our flesh, indulging the desires of the flesh and of the mind, and were by nature children of wrath, even as the rest."

This moral decay pervades every aspect of human behavior so that the lists of Rom.3.10-18, Eph.2.1-3, and Gal.5.19-21 summarized below indicate what Scripture says about the moral condi-

Man's moral decay

Rom.3.10-18	Eph.2.1-3	Gal. 3.19-21
• None righteous	• Walked according to Satan's dictates	• I\mmorality
• None who understands		• Impurity
• None who seek God	• Lived in the lust of the flesh	• Sensuality,
• All have turned aside		• Idolatry
• All have become useless	• Indulged the desires of the flesh and mind	• Sorcery
• No one does good		• Enmities
• Their mouth is an open grave		• Strife
• Their tongues deceive		• Jealousy
• The poison of asps is under their lips		• Outbursts of anger
•Their mouths are full of cursing and bitterness		• Disputes
•Their feet are swift to shed blood		• Dissensions
• Destruction and misery are in their paths		• Factions,
• The paths of peace they have not known		•
• There is no fear of God before their eyes.		• Drunkenness
		• Carousing,

tions of man. Moral decay invades and pervades the human race since Adam. Man will die physically, is separated from God and morally bankrupt, but there is one more consequence of death: Eternal death.

Eternal death

Eternal death means that man is forever separated from God and will spend eternity in the Lake of Fire prepared for Satan and his angels.[57] God is Holy and separate from sin. God is righteous and just and He must punish sin. He prepared the Lake of Fire for the devil and his angels, but after the Great White Throne judgment that follows the Battle of Gog-Magog, He will judge the nations and assign all unbelievers to that place of judgment.

God is merciful and gracious; but sin cannot remain unpunished, and so, after assigning unbelievers their punishment, God will cleanse the universe of the effects of sin. Peter tells us that God will destroy the heavens and earth down to the atom level[58] and then create new heavens and earth.

The only remedy for sinful mankind is found in redemption through Jesus Christ. All who believe and submit to His lordship receive forgiveness, cleansing, a new nature, the indwelling of the Holy Spirit, deliverance from Satan's control, and a future with

---

[57] Mat 25:41- "Then He will also say to those on His left, 'Depart from Me, accursed ones, into the eternal fire which has been prepared for the devil and his angels;

[58] 2 Pet.3.10. The word for "elements" is stoicheion which means "any first thing, from which the others belonging to some series or composite whole take their rise." Since atoms are the first things that make up material atoms it most likely means to this level. (Thayer's Lexicon in e-sword)

Christ forever. It is only through Jesus Christ that anyone can escape the eternal consequences of sin. Jesus said He alone in the way of salvation. Paul states in Rom. 10:9-13 the Gospel message. If you have never trusted Christ, then don't put off that decision any longer.

> "...that if you confess with your mouth Jesus as Lord, and believe in your heart that God raised Him from the dead, you will be saved; for with the heart a person believes, resulting in righteousness, and with the mouth he confesses, resulting in salvation. For the Scripture says, "WHOEVER BELIEVES IN HIM WILL NOT BE DISAPPOINTED." For there is no distinction between Jew and Greek; for the same Lord is Lord of all, abounding in riches for all who call on Him; for "WHOEVER WILL CALL ON THE NAME OF THE LORD WILL BE SAVED."

God revealed His redemption plan in the Garden of Eden when God said to Satan,

> "And I will put enmity Between you and the woman, And between your seed and her seed; He shall bruise you on the head, And you shall bruise him on the heel." (Gen 3:15)

God's redemptive plan began in the Garden of Eden when God killed an animal and made clothing for Adam and Eve. An animal had to die to allow Adam and Eve to fellowship with God.

> "The LORD God made garments of skin for Adam and his wife, and clothed them." (Gen 3:21)

God's redemptive plan continues as He makes covenants with Noah and Abraham. I'll give those details in the next chapter.

CHAPTER 3

COVENANTS

(Genesis 5-50)

The word "covenant" is used 316 times in the Bible.[59] God made a number of covenants with Israel and individuals. These include the covenant with Noah, with Abraham, Isaac, and Jacob. The covenant with the nation of Israel at Sinai is called the Book of the Covenant and includes the 10 commandments, plus additional moral and civil regulations.

God made a covenant with David and God made another covenant with Israel called the "New Covenant" which involves salvation through Jesus Christ according to Hebrews 8.8-13. It is not my purpose to cover all the details of each of the covenants, but to give an overview of the two covenants mentioned in Genesis: the covenant with Noah and the covenant with Abraham.

THE COVENANT WITH NOAH (GEN.5-10)

Genesis 5 records the genealogy of the human race from Adam to Noah. Chapter 6 verses 6,7 say,

> "The LORD was sorry that He had made man on the earth, and He was grieved in His heart. The LORD said, "I will blot out man whom I have created from the face of the land, from man to animals to creeping things and to birds of the sky; for I am sorry that I have made them."

---

[59] 279 references are in the Old Testament, the remaining 37 references are in the New Testament

Men had grown exceedingly wicked and intermarriage between the godly line of Seth and the ungodly line of Cain corrupted the godly line.[60] Noah alone was righteous, so God chose to continue the race through Noah and destroy every other living thing upon the earth.

THE UNIVERSAL FLOOD

God instructs Noah to build an ark 450 ft long by 75 ft wide and 45 feet tall. Into this ark he took 7 pairs of clean animals and 2 pairs of unclean animals and all the food necessary to feed them.[61] Noah and his sons endured the taunts of those living around them as they built the ark. Because it had never rained, when Noah announced he was building a boat, the people laughed.

In Noah's 600th year God told him to enter the ark with his family. Eight people and the selected animals entered the ark and God closed the door of the ark. They waited for 7 days until God caused the rain to fall and the fountains of the deep to burst open in the 2nd month on the 17th day of the month.[62] The rain fell for 40 days and 40 nights. The waters covered the entire earth and rose about 23 feet above the mountains.

"The water prevailed more and more upon the earth, so that all the high mountains everywhere under the heavens were covered.

---

[60] Many commentators believe these unions were between demons and women that produce Nephilim, or giants.

[61] The total cubic volume would have been 1,518,000 cubic feet [462,686.4 cubic meters] --that would be equal to the capacity of 569 modern railroad stock cars http://christiananswers.net/q-eden/edn-c013.html

[62] Gen.7.11

The water prevailed fifteen cubits higher, and the mountains were covered.' (Gen 7:19-20)[63]

The effects of a universal flood were devastating to the earth. Henry Morris, a hydrologist,[64] in his book "The Genesis Flood" chronicles the effects of the flood as the extreme pressures of the water rearranged the topography of the earth. The water remained on the earth for 150 days.[65]

About 3 months later the tops of the mountains became visible on the 1st day of the 10th month. 40 days later Noah released a raven which never returned to the ark. Then Noah sent out a dove that returned to the ark because it could find no food. 7 days later Noah sent out the dove again and this time it came back with an olive leaf. When he released the dove 7 days later, it never returned to the ark.

GOD'S COVENANT AND THE SIGN OF THE RAIN-BOW

Noah removed the covering from the top of the ark in the 601st year on the 1st day of the 1st month. In the 2nd month on the 27th day God instructed Noah and his family to leave the ark. The earth was dry.[66] Noah's first act was to build an altar and sacrifice one of

---

[63]The height of Mt. Ararat where the ark eventually landed is about 17,000 feet. (Gen.8.4). This means that this was not a local flood but a universal flood

[64] A hydrologist studies the physical properties of the earth's water systems by performing extensive field and laboratory research. He or she may study the role of water in an ecosystem, measure the amount of rainfall in a certain area, or test water samples to determine the presence of pollutants. http://www.wisegeek.com/what-does-a-hydrologist-do.htm

[65]Gen.8.3

each clean animal and bird to the Lord.[67] The Lord responded to Noah's sacrifice with a promise.

> "The LORD smelled the soothing aroma; and the LORD said to Himself, "I will never again curse the ground on account of man, for the intent of man's heart is evil from his youth; and I will never again destroy every living thing, as I have done. "While the earth remains, Seedtime and harvest, And cold and heat, And summer and winter, And day and night Shall not cease." (Gen 8:21-22)

Note that God's covenant [68] includes several provisions. First God promises to never again destroy the earth by a flood to punish man's sinfulness. This is a promise that preserves life in spite of man's continued resistance and rebellion against God. Rather than destroying mankind again, Rom.1.24 says He gave them over to practice their sinfulness.

> "Therefore God gave them over in the lusts of their hearts to impurity, so that their bodies would be dishonored among them."

The word "gave them over" is a word used when a prisoner is handed over for sentencing. Thayer says it means "…to deliver up one to custody, to be judged, condemned, punished, scourged, tormented, put to death."[69] Note what man has become, and what God "has given man over to" according to Rom.1.25-32. The list on the next page shows the depravity of man's heart, and only God's covenant with Noah keeps God from again destroying man.

---

[66] Gen.8.14-18

[67] Gen.8.20

[68] Gen.9.8-17 repeats this promise and calls it a covenant.

[69] Thayer's lexicon in e-sword. The word is used 136 times in the New Testament and is translated "betray, betrayed" 22 times, "deliver, deliver over" 21 times, "gave over or hand over or turn over" 23 times

- To impurity
- Degrading passions of homosexuality, lesbianism
- A depraved mind
- Unrighteousness
- Wickedness
- Greed
- Evil
- Envy
- Murder
- Strife
- Deceit
- Malice
- Gossips
- Slanderers
- Haters of God
- Insolent
- Arrogant
- Boastful
- Inventors of evil
- Disobedient to parents
- Without understanding
- Unloving
- Unmerciful
- Approving evil

A significant consequence is that God now starts over with Noah. It is only God's mercy and grace that keeps God from once again destroying sinful man.

Second, God promises Noah that He will continue the seasons without interruption. The flood changed not only the geographical arrangement of the earth, but the tropical climate of the earth prior to the flood. Prior to the flood, an atmospheric "canopy" surrounded the earth, but that canopy is now gone as God opens the floodgates of the sky.[70] God gave Noah the rainbow as a sign of the covenant as His promise to never again destroy the earth by a flood. God calls this covenant an "everlasting" covenant.

> "I establish My covenant with you; and all flesh shall never again be cut off by the water of the flood, neither shall there again be a flood to destroy the earth." God said, "This is the sign of the covenant which I am making between Me and you and every living creature that is with you, for all successive generations; I set My bow in the cloud, and it shall be for a sign of a covenant between Me and the earth. "It shall come about, when I bring a cloud over the earth, that the bow will be seen in the cloud, and I will remember My covenant, which is between Me and you and every living creature of all flesh; and never again shall the water become

[70] Gen.7.11. See "The Genesis Flood" by Henry Morris for a discussion of the pre-flood climate of the earth.

a flood to destroy all flesh. "When the bow is in the cloud, then I will look upon it, to remember the everlasting covenant between God and every living creature of all flesh that is on the earth." And God said to Noah, "This is the sign of the covenant which I have established between Me and all flesh that is on the earth." (Gen 9:11-17)

Noah lived 350 years after the flood for a total of 950 years.[71] Genesis 10 records the generations of Noah's 3 sons, Shem, Ham, Japheth. Chapter 11 records the building of the tower of Babel and explains that God stopped the building by confusing their language so they could not understand one another.

As a result men separated into different language groups as God scattered them across the face of the whole earth.[72] Genesis repeats Shem's godly line from Shem to Abraham, the man to whom God will make the next covenant. The line of Shem contains the following men.

The godly line through Noah's son Shem

Father	Age when his son was born	Son's name
Shem	100	Arpachshad
Arpachshad	35	Shelah
Shelah	30	Eber
Eber	34	Peleg
Peleg	30	Reu
Reu	32	Serug
Serug	30	Nahor
Nahor	29	Terah
Terah	70	Abram, Nahor, Haron

THE COVENANT WITH ABRAHAM (GEN. 11-50)

Terah's son, Haran, died in Ur of the Chaldeans sometime after the birth of his son, Lot, and the birth of his 2 daughters,

---

[71] Gen.9.28,29

[72] Gen.11.9

Milcah and Iscah. Abram married Sarai and Nahor married Haran's daughter, Milcah, in Ur.[73] Ur was identified by Charles Wolley in 1927 as a Sumerian city named Ur (modern *Tell el-Mukayyar*)." [74] However, the location of the city is still under discussion today.

The Call of Abraham

God called Abraham to leave Ur of the Chaldeans.[75] His father Terah, his brothers Haran and Nahor, and his nephew Lot, with their families, also made the journey. The entourage stopped in Haran where Terah died. God told Abram to go to Canaan where God would bless him and make him a great nation. Abram was 75 years old when he left Haran.[76]

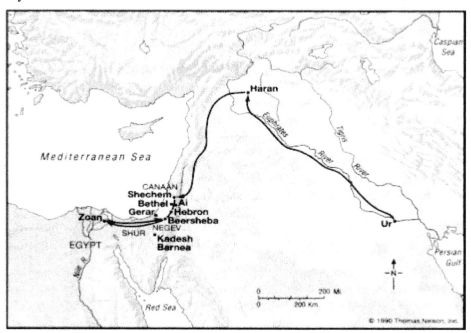

---

[73] Gen.11.27-32

[74] http://creationwiki.org/Ur_of_the_Chaldees

Abram made the journey as far as Shechem where God promised to give him the land. He built an altar and then went to Bethel where he built another altar. From Bethel Abram journeyed south into the land of the Negev, but since there was a famine in the land he continued to Egypt. Pharaoh gave Abram sheep, oxen, donkeys, camels and male and female servants. The reason for this Egyptian generosity is found in Gen.12.14-16.

> "It came about when Abram came into Egypt, the Egyptians saw that the woman was very beautiful. Pharaoh's officials saw her and praised her to Pharaoh; and the woman was taken into Pharaoh's house. Therefore he treated Abram well for her sake; and gave him sheep and oxen and donkeys and male and female servants and female donkeys and camels.

Sarai was a beautiful woman and Abram was fearful the Egyptians would kill him and take his wife. Abram and Sarai made a pact that she would say she was his sister. While this was partly true,[77] the deception and intent was a lie. However, God struck Pharaoh and his household with a plague.

Pharaoh asked Abram why he had lied about Sarai being his wife, and after Abram told him of his fears, the Pharaoh sent Abram out of Egypt, God removed the plague, and Abram, now a rich man,[78] settled in Bethel. Since that part of the land could not sustain the herds of both Abram and his nephew, Lot, Abram told Lot to

---

[75] The map is from Nelson's Bible charts and maps in e-sword

[76] Gen.12.4

[77] Gen.20.12 "Besides, she actually is my sister, the daughter of my father, but not the daughter of my mother, and she became my wife..." Unfortunately, Abram did not learn his lesson in Egypt for he told the same lie for the same reason to Abimelech a few years later.

[78] Gen.13.2

choose a place to live, and he would go the other direction. Lot chose to live near the cities of Sodom and Gomorrah in the Jordan valley. Abram settled in Canaan.[79] It is at this time that God made His covenant with Abram.

THE COVENANT INSTITUTED (GEN.11-20)

The covenant with Abraham is a unilateral covenant which means that only one party is responsible for the terms of the covenant. That party is God. He alone will honor the terms of the covenant.

The Abrahamic covenant is found in several passages in Genesis. It is first called a "promise"[80] but later becomes a formal covenant between God and Abram in Gen.15.1-21. It is reaffirmed and additional details are given in Gen.17.1-22.

Abraham's suggestion to God (Gen.15.1-6)

Since Abram is childless, he does not understand how God's words could come true, so he asks God that his servant Eliezer be his heir. God responds that Eliezer will not be his heir, but that one "from your own body, he shall be your heir."[81] God tells Abram his descendents will be as numerous as the stars of the heavens."[82] Abram believes God and it is reckoned to him as righteousness.[83]

---

[79] Gen.13.8-12

[80] Gen.12.1-3, 13.14-17

[81] Gen.15.4

[82] Gen.15.5

[83] Gen.15.6. Abram's faith is referred to several times in Scripture.

Sarah's sinful attempt to fulfill the cove nant (Gen.16)

In a vision God told Abram that his descendents would be enslaved 400 years, but God would deliver them, and they would return to the land God promised them. Since God had only specified that one "from his own body" would be his heir, after 10 years Sarai, who remained childless, suggested that Abram have a child by Hagar her servant.

Abram listened to Sarai. A year later Ishmael was born.[84] However, man's attempts to help God's plans never succeed, and Sarai became jealous of Hagar and cast her out into the desert. Only God's intervention prevented Ishmael's death.[85] Because he was Abram's son, God would bless Ishmael, but he would not be Abram's heir.

THE CUTTING OF THE COVENANT (GEN.15.1-22)

"Cutting the covenant" was the method in the Old Testament whenever a binding covenant was made.[86] God made the covenant with Abram after he rescued Lot and his family who had been taken from Sodom by 4 kings. They made war against the kings of Sodom, Gomorrah, Admah, and Zoar. Abram took his 318 trained men,

---

Rom.4.3,9,22, Gal.3.6, and Ja.2.23

[84] Abram was 86 years old (Gen.16.16

[85] Gen.16.9-14

[86] "The Hebrew **berith** means primarily *"a cutting"*, with reference to the custom of cutting or dividing animals in two and passing between the parts in ratifying a covenant." (Smith's Dictionary, "Covenant" in e-sword)

pursued the 4 kings from Mamre to Dan where he and his men surprised the enemy, and chased them all the way to Hobah, north of Damascus.[87]

Returning home with the spoils, Abram met Melchizedek, king of Salem (Jerusalem) and priest of God, to whom Abram paid a 10th of the spoils.[88] Abram rightly refused to accept anything from the king of Sodom, and said to him,

> "Abram said to the king of Sodom, "I have sworn to the LORD God Most High, possessor of heaven and earth, that I will not take a thread or a sandal thong or anything that is yours, for fear you would say, 'I have made Abram rich.' "I will take nothing except what the young men have eaten, and the share of the men who went with me, Aner, Eshcol, and Mamre; let them take their share." (Gen 14:22-24)

God later spoke to Abram in a vision and said,

> "After these things the word of the LORD came to Abram in a vision, saying, "Do not fear, Abram, I am a shield to you; Your reward shall be very great." (Gen 15:1)

When Abram asks for confirmation of God's promise, God instructs him to bring a 3 year old heifer, a 3 year old female goat, and a 3 year old ram, plus a turtledove and a young pigeon. Abram killed the animals and cut the heifer, goat, and ram into 2 pieces and laid the pieces apart from each other.

After the sun set, God walked through the path between the separated animal parts in the form of a smoking oven and flaming torch which legally "cut" the covenant. Since only God walked through the path, God alone would keep the covenant. (Gen.15.19-

---

[87] Gen.14.1-15

[88] Gen.14.16-20

21). If this had been a covenant with mutual requirements, then Abram and God would have both walked the path.

The sign of the covenant: circumcision (Gen.17.10-14,23-27)

God set the nation of Israel apart from all nations through the rite of circumcision which God instituted as the sign of the covenant.[89] Every male was circumcised at 8 days and anyone not circumcised was "cut off" from Israel.[90] Circumcision becomes the sign of inclusion into the nation of Israel, but does not demonstrate salvation. God expected the nation to follow Abraham's faith.

The "seal" of Abraham's faith (Rom.4.11)

Circumcision was not a sign of salvation because it excluded all females. After making the point that Abram was credited with righteousness prior to being circumcised, Paul in Romans 4.11, calls circumcision a "seal" of Abram's faith that makes him the "father" of spiritual children who have faith in God. All who believe in God's

---

[89] There is confusion and inconsistency among historians about the beginning of circumcision. Sixth Dynasty (2345–2181 BC) tomb artwork in Egypt is thought to be the oldest documentary evidence of circumcision, the most ancient depiction being a bas-relief from the necropolis at Saqqara (ca. 2400 BC) with the inscriptions reading: "The ointment is to make it acceptable." and "Hold him so that he does not fall". In the oldest written account, by an Egyptian named Uha, in the 23rd century BC, he describes a mass circumcision and boasts of his ability to stoically endure the pain: "When I was circumcised, together with one hundred and twenty men...there was none thereof who hit out, there was none thereof who was hit, and there was none thereof who scratched and there was none thereof who was scratched." While circumcision may have been practiced prior to Abram, it became a national requirement as a distinctive sign of God's covenant with Israel. (http://en.wikipedia.org/wiki /History_of_male_circumcision)

[90] Gen.17.14

promises and exercise faith as Abram did, and believe in God who raised Christ from the dead, are Abram's spiritual children.

Abraham blesses the world as men and women follow his faith. This aspect of the covenant is especially significant to Gentiles who believe in Christ.

The significance of the covenant summarized (Gen.15,17)

Paul says God will bless the world through Abraham's descendents who demonstrate faith in God. Thus the covenant with Abram has both national and spiritual benefits which I'll summarize next. There are three main provisions to the covenant. None of these provisions have been fully fulfilled to date. There are partial fulfillments in all three areas, but final fulfillment awaits the return of Christ.

1. To become a great nation

God told Abram in Gen.15,

"... "Now look toward the heavens, and count the stars, if you are able to count them." And He said to him, "So shall your descendants be." (Gen 15:5)

Gen.17.2 adds "...I will multiply you exceedingly," and verse 4 says "...you will be the father of a multitude of nations," and verse 6 says "...I will make you exceedingly fruitful, and I will make nations of you, and kings will come forth from you. " Abram means, "a high father"[91] but God now changes his name to "Abraham" which means "father of a multitude."[92]

---

[91] JFB and K&D commentaries e-sword

God also changed Sarai's name, which means "my princess"[93] to "Sarah" which means simply "princess."[94] Both name changes reflect their new positions as heads of a great nation.

In addition, God informs Abraham that Sarah, his 90 year old wife, will have a son the next year. Both Abraham and Sarah laugh at God's word, knowing Sarah is beyond child-bearing years, but they find 9 months later that God's word is true. Isaac is born and the nation now numbers 3 persons.[95]

2. To have a land of their own

Gen.15.18 says God gave Abram all the land "From the river of Egypt as far as the great river, the river Euphrates..." Gen.17.8 says God gave Abram all the land of Canaan. Abraham died at 175 years of age and never owned any land other than the cave of Machpelah which he bought from Ephron the Hittite for 400 shekels of silver.[96]

3. To bless the world

God promises Abram in Gen.12.3,

"And I will bless those who bless you, And the one who curses you I will curse. And in you all the families of the earth will be blessed." (Gen 12:3)

This part of the covenant is fulfilled through the Gospel as those who practice faith in God and in His Son Jesus Christ are

---

[92] Ibid.

[93] K&D in e-sword

[94] MacArthur in e-sword

[95] See Endnote 3 for a detailed chart of Abraham's line

[96] Gen.23

blessed through Abraham's seed: Christ. Paul uses this argument in
Galatians 3.8 and quotes Gen.12.3.

> "The Scripture, foreseeing that God would justify the Gentiles by
> faith, preached the gospel beforehand to Abraham, saying, "ALL
> THE NATIONS WILL BE BLESSED IN YOU." (Gal 3:8)

Paul quotes from Gen.12.7 in Gal.3.16 and bases his argument on the word "seed" used in the singular form to demonstrate
that God always intended the spiritual blessings of the Abrahamic
covenant to come through Christ. In Gal.3.29 Paul concludes that all
who believe in Christ are Abraham's descendents according to
God's promise. That brings us to a discussion of the fulfillment of
God's covenant with Abraham. I've stated that the covenant made
with Abraham was not fulfilled in Abraham's day. So that begs the
question, "When was it fulfilled?"

THE COVENANT FULFILLED (GEN.21-50, REV.20)

God's covenant begins with Abraham, but is not fulfilled
until after the second coming of Jesus Christ. God's plan continues
through Isaac and his son Jacob, but is not finally fulfilled until after
the return of Christ to the earth. This section explains the process
God used to fulfill His promises to Abraham.

The initial fulfillment of the covenant
(Gen.21-50)

God sovereignly chose that He would bring the fulfillment
of His covenant through Isaac rather than Ishmael. Genesis continues to demonstrate that a sovereign God makes choices based upon
His plan, not man's desires.

1. The covenant through Isaac

God promised Abraham that his son Isaac would be born to Sarah and that word was fulfilled in Gen.21.1,2 when Isaac was born.

a. The birth and sacrifice of Isaac (Gen.21,22)

Sarah was 90 and Abraham was 100 when Isaac was born. Abraham circumcised Isaac at 8 days just as God commanded. Sarah once again became jealous of Hagar when Isaac was weaned and she sent Hagar away. This time God permitted Abraham to listen to Sarah and promised that Ishmael would become a great nation.[97]

When Isaac was a young man, God commanded Abraham to sacrifice Isaac on Mt. Moriah. Though this was against everything that Abraham believed, he obeyed God. Hebrews 11.19 tells us that Abraham believed God would raise Isaac from the dead.

> "He considered that God is able to raise people even from the dead, from which he also received him back as a type." (Heb 11:19)

God was testing Abraham according to both Gen.22.1 and Heb.11.17. Abraham passed God's test and God again repeated his promise to Abraham.

> "...and said, "By Myself I have sworn, declares the LORD, because you have done this thing and have not withheld your son, your only son, indeed I will greatly bless you, and I will greatly multiply your seed as the stars of the heavens and as the sand which is on the seashore; and your seed shall possess the gate of their enemies. "In your seed all the nations of the earth shall be blessed, because you have obeyed My voice." (Gen 22:16-18)

---

[97] Gen.21.12,13

b. Isaac's marriage to Rebekah and his sons Esau and Jacob

Because Abraham did not want Isaac to intermarry with the Canaanites, he had his servant go back to his country to find a wife for Isaac.[98]

(1) His marriage

The story of how God provided Rebekah, daughter of Laban, nephew of Abraham, as Isaac's wife is told in Gen.24. Isaac was 40 when he married Rebekah.[99]

(2) The birth of Esau and Jacob

20 years later, after Isaac prayed for his barren wife to have children, Esau and Jacob where born when Abraham was 160 years old. The nation God promised to Abraham now numbers 4 people: Abraham, Isaac, Rebekah, and Jacob.[100]

c. The confirmation of the covenant to Isaac (Gen.26)

Abraham died at 175. Isaac and Ishmael buried him with Sarah in the cave of Machpelah.[101] When a famine came upon the land, Isaac purposed to go to Egypt, but God appeared to Isaac and told him not to go to Egypt, so Isaac stayed in the land of the

---

[98] Gen.24.1-4

[99] Gen.25.20. Abraham would be 140 years old.

[100] Esau and Ishmael are not included because the line of promise goes through Isaac.

[101] Gen.25.7-10

Philistines. God said He would bless him, and He repeated the covenant provisions made to Abraham.

> "Sojourn in this land and I will be with you and bless you, for to you and to your descendants I will give all these lands, and I will establish the oath which I swore to your father Abraham. "I will multiply your descendants as the stars of heaven, and will give your descendants all these lands; and by your descendants all the nations of the earth shall be blessed; because Abraham obeyed Me and kept My charge, My commandments, My statutes and My laws." (Gen 26:3-5)

2. The covenant through Jacob (Gen.27-36)

When Rebekah delivered the twins, Esau and Jacob, God told Isaac,

> "The LORD said to her, "Two nations are in your womb; And two peoples will be separated from your body; And one people shall be stronger than the other; And the older shall serve the younger." (Gen 25:23)

Choosing the younger instead of the firstborn overturned the cultural norm. The firstborn had the rights of privilege. A sovereign God has the right to determine to bless whomever He chooses.[102] Unfortunately, Jacob tried several ways to help God's statement come true. Through deceptive means, Jacob first stole Esau's birthright when he sold lentil stew to a famished Esau just returning from a hunting expedition.[103]

Second, when Rebekah heard Isaac request a meal of game from Esau so that he could bestow his blessing on him before he died, she conspired with Jacob to trick Isaac into giving the blessing to Jacob. She prepared a meal, dressed Jacob in Esau's clothes, and put goat skin on his smooth arms to make them appear hairy.

---

[102] Rom.9.10-16

[103] Gen.25.29-34

Jacob impersonated Esau, and received the blessing from his father. However, Jacob so angered his brother Esau that Rebekah sent Jacob to her father's home to keep Esau from killing him

a. The covenant reaffirmed through Jacob

Jacob left for Haran with the blessing of Isaac and had a dream at a place he called "Bethel- house of God." There God reaffirmed the covenant He made with Abraham and applied it to Jacob and his descendents.

> "He had a dream, and behold, a ladder was set on the earth with its top reaching to heaven; and behold, the angels of God were ascending and descending on it. And behold, the LORD stood above it and said, "I am the LORD, the God of your father Abraham and the God of Isaac; the land on which you lie, I will give it to you and to your descendants. "Your descendants will also be like the dust of the earth, and you will spread out to the west and to the east and to the north and to the south; and in you and in your descendants shall all the families of the earth be blessed. "Behold, I am with you and will keep you wherever you go, and will bring you back to this land; for I will not leave you until I have done what I have promised you." (Gen 28:12-15)

God had a plan for Jacob that included going to Laban's home where he would spent 20 years working for Rebekah's brother, Laban. Jacob married Rachel and Leah, had many sons and daughters, gained large herds, and at the end of 20 years left Laban's home to return to his father, Isaac, who was living in Hebron.[104]

Jacob heard that Esau was coming to meet him with 400 men. The night before the meeting, God met with Jacob and wrestled with him until dawn.[105] When Jacob demanded a blessing, God changed his name from "Jacob," which means either "heel-catcher"

---

[104] Gen.35.27

[105] Gen.32.24-32

or "deceiver,"[106] to "Israel," which means "God's fighter," or "he struggles with God."[107]

After an amicable reunion with Esau,[108] Jacob moved to Shechem where he bought a piece of land from Hamor. Jacob's daughter, Dinah, went to visit some girls in the city of Shechem and was raped by Hamor's son Shechem.

When Hamor approached Jacob to request Dinah marry his son, Jacob's sons intervened and said they could not allow their sister to marry an uncircumcised man. Hamor agreed to circumcise all the men of the city and Simeon and Levi, Jacob's sons, killed all the men while they were healing and unable to fight.

God tells Jacob to move to Bethel and once there, God appeared again to Jacob and reaffirmed that his name was now Israel. God also reaffirmed the covenant with him.[109] He promised to make Jacob a great nation, and give him the land promised to Abraham. Rachel died on the journey giving birth to Benjamin.[110] The nation of Israel now consists of Jacob, 12 sons, and 1 daughter.[111]

b. Jacob's move to Egypt

God had promised Abraham that he would be the father of a great nation. That nation consists of about 14 people at this point.

---

[106] MacArthur's commentary in e-sword

[107] Ibid.

[108] Gen.34

[109] Gen.35.9-13

[110] Gen.35.18. Rachel died in Bethlehem

[111] I did not include Jacob's wives Bilhah and Zilpah since their sons are seen as Leah's and Rachel's children.

Jacob was 108 years old when Joseph was sold as a slave in Egypt by his jealous brothers,[112] and Jacob was 120 years old when his father Isaac died.[113]

(1) Joseph sent ahead to prepare a place

Abraham's nation of 14 people does not begin to meet God's promise of a great nation. But whenever we think God has forgotten His promises, just at that time God begins to move. We get impatient and frustrated when God does not move according to our schedule. But remember that God is never late– He is always just in time.

Ps.105.17 tells us that God sent Joseph to Egypt as a slave to prepare a place for Jacob to develop into a great nation and fulfill the promise God made to Abraham. God tested Joseph by afflicting him with fetter and irons until God was ready to promote Joseph as 2nd in command of all of Egypt.

> "He sent a man before them, Joseph, who was sold as a slave. They afflicted his feet with fetters, He himself was laid in irons; Until the time that his word came to pass, The word of the LORD tested him. " (Psa 105:17-19

Joseph spent 13 years from the time he went to Egypt until he was promoted to the throne. We do not know how long Joseph was a servant at Potipher's home, or his stay in prison, although we do know that he was in prison 2 years after interpreting the baker's and butler's dreams.[114]

---

[112] Gen.37.2

[113] Gen.35.28 (Jacob was born when Isaac was 60)

[114] Gen.41.1

God's timing is always perfect and God gives Pharaoh a dream his wise men could not interpret. The cupbearer suddenly loses his amnesia and remembers Joseph who interpreted his dream! They call for Joseph in prison and God enables him not only to interpret Pharaoh's dream, but also to present a practical solution to the coming years of plenty and the years of famine. Pharaoh immediately promotes Joseph to 2nd in command of Egypt.

(2) Israel grows into a great nation

Joseph is now in a position to fulfill God's promise to Abraham that his people would be slaves for 400 years, but then be delivered.[115] Joseph, however, is unaware of God's plan for his life. During the 7 years of plenty Joseph builds storage cities for the grain he collects for the lean years ahead.

Two years into the lean years, Joseph's brothers stand before Joseph to buy grain. The brothers do not recognize Joseph, but he recognizes them, and decides to test their hearts. After accusing them of being spies, Joseph puts them in prison for 3 days, then keeps Simeon while the remaining brothers return home to bring Benjamin to Egypt.

In spite of the protests of Jacob, the brothers return for more grain after Judah accepts responsibility for Benjamin's safety. Upon reaching Egypt, they return the money found in their sacks after the first visit, and are surprised when they are invited to dine with Egypt's rule (Joseph). Joseph instructs his steward to put his silver

---

[115] Gen.15.13,14

cup in Benjamin's sack and the men leave for home, unaware of what Joseph has done.

When the silver cup is found in Benjamin's sack, the discouraged men return to Joseph's home unsure of what is about to happen. Joseph confronts his brothers with their deed and they confess that God is punishing them for their selling Joseph.[116] Judah pleads with Joseph to allow him to stay in place of Benjamin since he had pledged himself to protect his brother. At this point Joseph clears the room and reveals he is their brother Joseph.

After tears of joy, surprise and sorrow, Joseph introduces his brothers to Pharaoh who instructs Joseph to give his brothers wagons to bring his father and family to Egypt to live. Thus Jacob comes to Egypt at 130 years of age. God's plan to grow this small nation of 70 plus people into a great nation has begun! 430 years later, God will deliver Israel from Egypt by 10 plagues under the leadership of Moses. Volume 2 of "The Amazing Journey Series" tells the story of the exodus from Egypt and Joshua's conquest of the land in a book I've titled, "Foundations."

The final fulfillment: the Millennial kingdom (Rev.20)

One final issue is necessary to close this chapter properly. God promised Abraham, a land, a people, and a blessing to the world. The blessing to the world comes by redemption through Jesus Christ, which is the purpose for the story of the Bible. The

---

[116] Judah may have been remembering his sin of adultery and his mistreatment of Tamar and subsequent adultery with her (Gen.38)

people grew into a great nation in Egypt and have multiplied over the centuries even though various dictators have tried to annihilate them.

The one remaining promise is the land. Even though Israel became an official nation-state in 1948, they do not yet posses the land that God promised them in Gen.15.18, ""To your descendants I have given this land, From the river of Egypt as far as the great river, the river Euphrates."

God will fulfill this part of the covenant, to give Israel their land, after the Rapture of the Body of Christ and the subsequent 7 year tribulation. Jesus Christ returns at the end of that 7 year period to earth, puts Satan and his demons in prison in the Pit, and sets up His 1,000 year reign upon the earth.[117]

---

[117] For a complete discussion of the book of Revelation you may find my book titled "EPILOGUE: The Consummation of God's eternal plan" found on Amazon.com written under my pen name Pastor John Davis.

Summary

Genesis is the book of beginnings as God chooses, according to His sovereign will and plan, to create all that exists, permit sin to enter the world, and sets in motion the plan that will redeem those He chooses. This survey of Genesis assumes the truthfulness of God's revelation in Scripture and the right of a sovereign God to do as He chooses. Genesis teaches us that a right relationship with God demands we submit to God's will; resisting God's will results in condemnation and loss.

CREATION

God is the Creator; we are the created. This is a clear theme in Genesis. God created *ex nihilo,* "out of nothing," in six literal 24-hour days. No other explanation adequately explains the intricacies of our bodies, our world and the universe. The faulty assumptions of scientists unwilling to submit to the moral dictates of a sovereign God forces them to develop untenable theories that not only fail to explain where we came from, but also demand more faith than believing in a sovereign Creator!

God loves and cares for His creation, but He also expects His creation to glorify Him. Satan held the highest position among the angels, yet he desired more and lost everything. God put Adam and Eve in a perfect environment with every need met, yet they desired more and lost everything. Paul's statement in 1 Timothy 6 summarizes our need.

"But godliness actually is a means of great gain when accompanied by contentment. (1Ti 6:6)

Years ago someone gave me a card that tells us how to find contentment if we practice its truth.

"When for the first time in your life you realize that all you have is God; then for the first time in your life you will understand that all you need is God."

Corruption and condemnation

God tested Adam and Eve in the Garden of Eden by giving them only one prohibition: "Do not eat of the tree of the knowledge of good and evil in the middle of the Garden." Satan cunningly appealed to Eve's emotions, and she ate of the fruit and gave some to Adam who willingly chose to disobey the direct command of God.

The results were catastrophic not only for Adam and Eve, but for the human race.. Immediate spiritual death, the beginning of the decay that leads to physical death, expulsion from the Garden, hard work to sustain life, extra pain in child-bearing, and ultimately, eternal separation from God in the Lake of Fire created to punish Satan and his demons. But for the mercy and grace of God, all people should suffer that fate, but a sovereign God, willing to demonstrate His mercy, chose to save some and set in motion His eternal plan to send Christ as the Redeemer.

Covenants

God's moral outrage and hatred of man's sin is seen clearly in Genesis 6 when He determines to destroy everything on the earth except 8 people. Noah builds an ark at God's command, and the water pressure of a world-wide flood rearranges the geography of the earth as water rises 23 feet above the highest mountain. For 150 days water ravages the earth until God allows it to recede.

God starts the human race over with Noah. He makes a covenant with Noah that He will never again destroy man by water. The sign of that promise is the rainbow we see after rain showers. The human race begins to multiply again through the family of Noah until God chooses a man called Abraham, born to Terah in Ur of the Chaldeans, to head the people through whom God's plan of redemption will come.

God calls Abraham to move from Ur to Canaan where He will make him a great nation, give him all the land from the Euphrates River to the Nile River, and bless the world through his descendent: Jesus Christ. That plan proceeds through the godly line of Isaac, his son Jacob and Jacob's 12 sons. Judah is the son through whom Jesus Christ will be born centuries later.

To grow Jacob's family into nation-size, God sends Joseph into slavery in Egypt and through God's sovereign superintendence promotes him to 2nd in command of all of Egypt. A famine brings Joseph's brothers to Egypt for food, and through a number of tests, Joseph determines his brothers are repentant of selling him into slavery. He brings his father and 70 people to Egypt in fulfillment of God's promise to Abraham that the nation would become slaves in a foreign land, but be delivered after 400 years.

The nation of Israel is God's chosen nation; Jacob is God's chosen line. God's plan of redemption is on the move. The books of

Exodus through Deuteronomy tell the story of God's provision of a land for His people. The remainder of the Old Testament tells the failure of Israel to obey God in spite of God's warnings through judges, prophets, and kings.

Yet God's plan moves forward until Jesus Christ is born in Bethlehem, dies on a Roman cross, and ascends to heaven to await the time when the Father tells him to bring His Church home. God the Father will fulfill His promises to Abraham and David 7 years after the Rapture of the Church when the Millennial reign of Christ begins.

Jesus Christ died on a Roman cross and rose from a borrowed tomb to sit on heaven's throne. While waiting for the day to bring the Church home, Christ is calling for people to repent and be saved. Have you responded to Christ? He promises "WHOEVER WILL CALL ON THE NAME OF THE LORD WILL BE SAVED."[118] Here is what is necessary for you to be saved.

> "...if you confess with your mouth Jesus as Lord, and believe in your heart that God raised Him from the dead, you will be saved; for with the heart a person believes, resulting in righteousness, and with the mouth he confesses, resulting in salvation." (Rom 10:9-10)

As Adam had a choice to eat of the fruit offered by Eve, so you have a choice to respond to God by confessing that Jesus is Lord, believing in your heart that God raised Him from the dead, and trusting Him as Lord of your life. What will your choice be?

---

[118] Rom 10:13

Endnotes

1-   55 references to 'bara' – 'to shape or create'

Gen. 1:1,21,27; 2:3,4; 5:1,2; 6:7; Exo. 34:10; Num. 16:30; Deu. 4:32; Jos. 17:15,18; Psa. 51:10; 89:12,47; 102:18; 104:30; 148:5; Ecc. 12:1; Isa. 4:5; 40:26,28; 41:20; 42:5; 43:1,7,15; 45:7,8,12,18; 48:7; 54:16; 57:19; 65:17,18; Jer. 31:22; Eze. 21:19,30; 23:47; 28:13,15; Amos 4:13; Mal. 2:10;

Genesis   8 verses found   11 matches

Exodus   1 verse found 1 match

Numbers   1 verse found 2 matches

Deuteronomy 1 verse found 1 match

Joshua   2 verses found   2 matches

Psalms   6 verses found   6 matches

Ecclesiastes   1 verse found 1 match

Isaiah   17 verses found   21 matches

Jeremiah   1 verse found 1 match

Ezekiel   5 verses found   7 matches

Amos   1 verse found 1 match

Malachi   1 verse found 1 match

2 The Days of Genesis

"The Hebrew Yom: Taking One Day at a Time, "
http://www.creationtoday.org/the-hebrew-yom-taking-one-day-at-a-time/

John C. Whitcomb, "The Bible and Astronomy,"

James Stambaugh, http://www.icr.org/article/288/,

Rodney Whitefield, http://godandscience.org/youngearth/yom_with_number.pdf

3- Abraham's Genealogy

Abraham's genealogy is given in detail on the chart on the next page. God gives just enough details to make such a chart possible so that we can see the involvement and inter-relationships of people. The chart on the following page shows the relationships and time sequences for Abraham's family. It is an interesting study to pursue.

Abraham's Genealogy

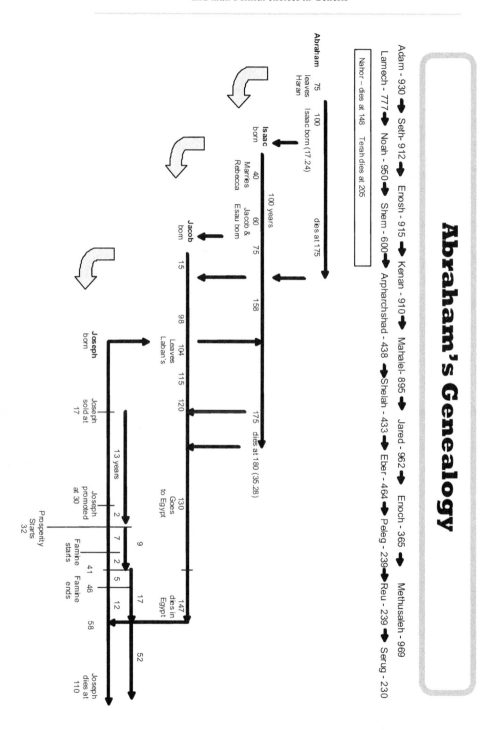

Adam - 930 ➡ Seth- 912 ➡ Enosh - 915 ➡ Kenan - 910 ➡ Mahalel- 895 ➡ Jared - 962 ➡ Enoch - 365 ➡ Methusaleh - 969

Lamech - 777 ➡ Noah - 950 ➡ Shem - 600 ➡ Arpharchshad - 438 ➡Shelah - 433 ➡ Eber - 464 ➡ Peleg - 239➡Reu - 239 ➡ Serug - 230

Nahor – dies at 148   Terah dies at 205

Abraham
leaves
Haran

75   100   dies at 175

Isaac born (17.24)

Isaac
born

40   60   75   158
Marries   Jacob &
Rebecca   Esau born

100 years

Jacob
born

15   98   104   115   120   175 dies at 180 (35.28)
Leaves
Laban's

Joseph
born

Joseph
sold at
17

130
Goes
to Egypt

13 years   2   7   9   2   5   17   147
dies in
Egypt

Joseph
promoted
at 30

Famine   Famine
starts   ends

41   46   58   52

Prosperity
Starts
32

Joseph
dies at
110

Printed in Great Britain
by Amazon

65541918R00058